THE NEW PAGAN HANDBOOK

By Pat Regan

This first edition published in 2008
By Lear Books
Windrush
High Tor West
Earl Shilton
Leics
LE9 7DN
England

www.learbooks.co.uk

The New Pagan Handbook © Pat Regan 2008.
Pat Regan has asserted his right under the Copyright, Designs and Patents Act 1988 to be identified as the author of this work.

All rights reserved. No part of this book may be used or reproduced in any form without written permission of the author, except in case of quotation in articles and reviews.

Cover artwork © Levanah
Cover design by Paul Mason

ISBN 978-0-9547534-5-0

Printed in England by Booksprint

CONTENTS

5	**INTRODUCTION – PAGANISM**
12	**CHAPTER ONE - THE SUBVERSION OF A RELIGION**
14	Freya's Cats
15	The Witch's Cat
15	Witchprickers
16	The Black Death
17	Propaganda
19	The Law Makers
19	The Wise Ones
21	Fundamentalism and Christianity
23	Hijacking Pagan Beliefs
28	Paganism got there First
30	**CHAPTER TWO – THE GODS**
31	The God Forms
32	The Fairies
35	The Gods in Dreams
36	Meditation
40	**CHAPTER THREE – RITUAL**
40	Preparing Sacred Space
41	The Purification Bath
41	The Rite of Self-Initiation
44	Consecrating Magical Tools
44	Rite for Self-cleansing and Protection
46	Seasonal Rites
48	**CHAPTER FOUR- MAGIC**
48	The Timing of Magic
49	The Athame
50	Spell Working
53	**CHAPTER FIVE- SEASONAL FESTIVALS**
53	Midsummer
54	Lughnasadh
55	Yuletide and the Saturnalia
56	January, New Year and the Compitalia

57	February, the Feralia and Terminalia
59	March
60	April, the Parilia, Vinalia and Veneralia
61	May, the Floralia and Beltane
63	**EPILOGUE**
65	**APPENDIX 1- A-Z of Roman Festivals**
71	**APPENDIX 2 – Jewels**
73	**APPENDIX 3 – Numbers**
75	**APPENDIX 4 – Symbols**
123	**APPENDIX 5 – Cards**
126	**ENDNOTES**

Introduction
PAGANISM

One of the most widely abused words in the English language today must surely be 'Pagan'. The term is given to mean, by various dictionaries, 'Heathen, Non-Christian, Moslem, Jewish or Buddhist'. It is also often a term used to vilify others as barbarians, thugs or merely unenlightened non-religious fools.

We get the term Pagan from the Latin *paganus*, meaning 'countryman.' The name 'Heathen' simply denotes one who dwells on a heath. Modern dictionary compilers can hardly plead ignorance to the fact that there is a fast-growing number of practicing Pagan folk in the U.K. Information regarding statistics on Pagan beliefs, customs and practices is now easy to obtain. Interested parties no longer need to accept defamatory third-hand propaganda on Paganism from religious trouble makers, journalists seeking scandal, or any other unhelpful zealots short on wits. For too long Paganism has suffered from negative connotations unjustly foisted on it by the early Church. The mediaeval witch stereotype of a green-faced hag on a broomstick is long past its sell by date. Images such as this may seem like fun to the small-minded but to many modern Pagans, who simply wish to lead quiet lives, they remain crude, immature and extremely offensive. Political correctness can sometimes be taken to extremes but just as many Jewish people would rightly object to being typecast in the mean old Fagin mould, Pagans too have sensitivities that can be sorely stretched at times.

In this book I shall attempt to enlighten the reader regarding the Pagan worldview and guide him or her into a different way of perceiving the place that they fill in this world, our home.

Modern Paganism and Heathenism has many different paths or, as some may prefer to call them, denominations. There are Druids, Odinists, Wiccans, witches and followers of shamanism amongst others. All paths are open to individual interpretation and expression because Paganism itself is not explicitly doctrinal. We Pagans believe strongly in individuality and the freedom to choose our own spiritual path through this life and beyond. The intolerance exhibited by monotheistic fundamentalists of any ilk is seen by enlightened Pagans as being repressive, worrying and ultimately very damaging to both the individual and society as a whole. The Pagan way is one of relating to nature's intimate cycles of which we are all a small but significant part. Pagans see themselves as being inherently interconnected with the natural scheme of things, not distant or opposed to it as is the case with uncompromising man-made religions.

Modern Paganism, like the pre-Christian faiths of our forebears, is Earth-orientated. This planet is our home and if we fail to care for it we shall reap a bitter harvest. This is no pie in the sky New Age fancy; common wisdom dictates that if any animal constantly fouls its own nest then it will only be a matter of time before illness and disease set in. On a larger scale, we are now beginning to see the frightening results of man's lack of respect and greed with intensive factory farming, acid rain, the destruction of rain forests, loss of native hedgerows and industrial pollution in both rural and urban areas and so on; the list is endless. While smiling politicians in grey suits tell us everything is just fine, rivers clog up with toxic waste from stinking abattoirs and over-loaded dairy farms. The grey-suits turn the other way as native oak, willow and alder come crashing to the ground. Multinational fast-food giants promote their unhealthy products to gullible consumers who don't see the link between intensive cattle rearing in distant countries and the rape of eco-systems. Governments merely look on as car pollution reaches critical levels instead of cutting their losses with the oil industries and ploughing some funds back into researching and developing alternative low-pollution battery and electric-powered motor vehicles.

Our ancient Pagan ancestors, unlike modern man, held the Earth and all its many inhabitants in high esteem. Most pre-Christian societies had pantheons of deities that co-existed very satisfactorily with gods and goddesses from other cultures, no matter how far away that particular culture might have been. Many important examples of this type of mythological harmonization have occurred throughout time. For instance, if we take the trouble to put almost any ancient deity under scrutiny we very quickly discover that he has one or more distinctly equivalent 'god-forms' in different societies. These are obviously cross-linked and filling the same, or at least a very similar, role in the spiritual scheme of things.

The table opposite is included to serve as an example of the wide variety of god-forms that parallel one another; it would be quite easy to substitute god-forms from many other cultures. Early man, in his natural wisdom, shared an ancient psychic heritage that spanned the whole globe regardless of barriers such as geographical location, cultural make-up, racial difference, tribal taboo, sociological configuration and linguistic constraints. These powerful thought-forms need to be examined very closely as they are central landmarks that must be heeded if we are ever going to pilot our mundane-conscious selves through the dark waters of mythological understanding.

Perceptions

The British Isles - with its rich blend of native customs, traditions, myths and legends - is without doubt one of the greatest starting places to explore our Pagan birthright. The many widely diverse peoples that invaded and inhabited this country shared a common psychic denominator. This gift (to call it less

	Celtic	Roman	Greek
God of Warfare	Lugh	Mars	Ares
Goddess of Love	Branwen	Venus	Aphrodite
Goddess of the Moon	Arianrhod	Diana	Hecate
God of the Underworld	Bile and Bel	Dis	Hades
Goddess of Flowers	Blodeuwedd	Flora	Chloris
God of the Sky	Nuada	Jupiter	Zeus
Goddess of Battles	Morrighan	Bellona	Eny'o
God of Healing	Diancecht	Aesculapius	Askelpius

would be to do a great disservice to the gods themselves) enabled the ancients to 'sidestep' ordinary everyday human consciousness and attain greater awareness of self. It allowed them to reach deeply into that mystical pool of wisdom where the individual human spirit connects with the whole spiritual matrix of the cosmos.

The communal aspect of this paranormal ability is by no means limited to humankind; on the contrary animals, birds, fish, insects and every other being in existence has the psychic ability to connect with neighbours of their own kind and sometimes other species too. Every autumn the majestic salmon defy all the odds and mysteriously find their way home to the headwaters of their birth. Racing pigeons perform a similar feat on a much more regular basis, often travelling vast distances to reach the suburban safety of the loft. The first frost of winter sees the strange migration of countless numbers of pink-footed and greylag geese. Their timely arrival must have been regarded as a sure sign, by our Celtic ancestors, of the necessity of getting the cattle down from the mountainside before winter's deadly grip marked out her victims.

This psychic ability in our animal cousins is well known to most cat and dog owners. How many owners have noticed their pooch suddenly get out of its bed, eyes wide and ears high, tail frantically wagging, just as they had, only moments before, mentally planned that walk around a local field?

Science is only just scratching the surface of the whys and wherefores of what Paganism has been saying about animals' supernatural abilities for ages. It's rather amusing to realise that after centuries of ridiculing 'magical' practices, scientists are now seeking to understand the inherent complexities of such seemingly paranormal events such as why, when their owners leave work, do some dogs suddenly get up and await their return, regardless of time and distance?

In many ways, yesterday's magic has become today's scientific fact; pioneers in experimental sciences are falling over themselves claiming 'new' discoveries in understanding how one level of reality inter-connects with others. So-called new finds in medicine and physics are often re-discoveries of ancient Pagan wisdom. Scientists have recently heralded the Australian tea-tree as a brilliant 'cure-all' with its usefulness against bacterial infections. What science doesn't tell us is that the Aborigines have been brewing up tea-tree for health reasons since the first hunter discovered that flint could crack a victim's skull. The same thing happened with aspirin, a painkiller originally extracted from willow bark. For centuries witches have produced infusions from this tree to heal headaches and quell heat in fevers. This scenario is repeated throughout history many times over. Virtually nothing is new under the sun, especially science's claim regarding the use of nature's bounty to cure mankind's ills. Contrary to what some people believe, genuine magical, Pagan systems of religious thought are very compatible with today's scientific ideas.

There now seems to be a significant shift in the cultural perception of the world of magic and myth. Gone are the days when the studious individual, hungry for 'hidden' knowledge, feared the bloody attentions of the Inquisition - although many contemporary theologians would still drag humankind back to the dark days of Galileo's *Examen Rigorosum*. It is not without good reason that religious minorities in society frequently have to remind fundamentalist politicians that we do, in fact, all live in a multi-faith, democratic society and that their own particular religious view certainly does not have ascendancy over other, less orthodox, beliefs. The illusion of this being a free country is soon breached the moment an individual or group of like-minded folk decide to worship divinity in an unorthodox fashion. Many innocent neo-Pagans have drawn attention, suspicion, mistrust and disdain, not by committing any illegal or wicked action but by simply daring to be individualistic in their mode of religious practice. A country is only as free as the people who dwell there.

One of the great attractions of Paganism is that it does away with the spiritual middleman. Every person on this planet has the human right to direct his or her own destiny through the sometimes difficult waters of spiritual exploration. The real liberation of self can never be achieved by leaving one's fate in the hands of others, no matter how trustworthy that individual may seem. The Pagan is his and her own priest or priestess, giving the spiritual overseer (essential in monotheistic faiths) the boot. Unlike many other belief-systems, Paganism does not proselytize. It is a spiritual path that recognises the needs of the individual. These needs, especially the spiritual ones, give humanity its wonderful diversity and without such differences we become shallow, uninspired, emotionally-sterile and eventually over-pious and fraudulent. Sadly, most of the evil in world history stems from one conquering religion seeking to suppress and destroy other faiths and force conformity on the masses. Diversity is a prime requisite of Paganism.

In response to the modern spiritual vacuum, growing numbers of freethinking people have filled it with a return to the native pre-Christian religions of their ancestors. Contemporary Paganism can trace its origins right back to the very dawn of civilisation. Unlike modern man-made religions, Paganism is of the earth, of the trees, of the sky and of the sea. It stands as a genuine mode of relating to, connecting with and experiencing - in many compelling and beautiful ways - the manifold, changing cosmic forces that affect us every single day of the year.

Unlike Christianity and other one-god belief systems, Paganism does not seek a messianic or saviour figure to save humanity from ruin. Modern Pagans, instead of looking for a scapegoat for their own faults, believe that an individual should take responsibility for his/her own conduct, errors, weaknesses and indiscretions. Laying the blame for one's actions on some other poor unfortunate is anathema to the Pagan who believes that such selfish behaviour stunts spiritual progress.

How will we ever learn (either individually or as a society) from our mistakes if we sit back, thinking all our evils will somehow be forgiven? This odd concept has, throughout the ages, given criminals unlimited licence to think they can do as they please. Why worry about today if one will be let off sins tomorrow? This has done, and will continue to do, grave damage to society. Then there's always old Satan to fall back on. *'The Devil has made me do it,'* has frequently been cried by wrongdoers hoping to escape justice. What we have here is nothing but a two way cop-out, a forgiving messianic deliver of sin on one hand, and a Satanic scapegoat to blame on the other.

The Pagan will have nothing to do with this type of negative, dualistic nonsense. If we commit a wrong deed then we must learn by it and/or face the consequences. A child touching a hot plate doesn't seek a scapegoat for its mistake; it screams and asks for aid then learns not to grab at the plate again in future. We must, like this child, learn from the errors of our ways instead of expecting others to take the blame for our own foolishness. The thinker who accepts the price for his/her actions does a very magical thing indeed and that is to develop a stronger, more unyielding will than the lesser mortal who cannot face the consequences of their own ignoble acts.

Our ancient Pagan ancestors, with their honour, camaraderie and loyalty to friend, family and tribal unit, give us an insight into the true meaning of taking responsibility for one's own affairs. The iron will of the ancients quietly stood firm in a native spiritual underground movement which is now resurfacing anew.

The current disenchantment of millions of people, especially the younger generation, with established orthodox belief-systems is now a great worry to the leaders of these faiths. The ecclesiastical authorities are pumping massive amounts of cash and resources into all manner of trendy advertising campaigns in order attract their failing congregations back to the fold. The vast number of alternative religions is seen as a great threat to the orthodox establishment. Modern newspaper columns are frequently filled with puerile and damaging anti-Pagan propaganda. Much of this is written by naïve people who have no knowledge of their own pre-Christian heritage and who are simply responding under the influence of their own religious indoctrination. However, there is another group of writers who are quite a different kettle of fish and much more dangerous to all religious minorities; we shall call them 'the experts'. These are well versed in their own twisted version of ancient history, seeing our Pagan ancestors as spiritual morons in need of a saviour to show them the true way. Unaware readers may take on board their fabrications as historical truths, leading to a subconscious prejudice against religious minorities, especially Pagans - and as we know, ignorance and bigotry often lead to hatred and violence.

Persecution of religious minorities is nothing new. Conquering cultures have always sought to convert or suppress competing philosophical and spiritual views. Our present culture is no exception to this law of human nature. Bigotry and prejudice usually starts early in life with the blind acceptance of social, racial, sexual or religious stereotyping and unthinking conformity. One group of individuals sees itself as being in some way superior and greater than another - Nazis over the Jews, Christians over the witches, etc. In the 1960s, Skinheads and Suedeheads soon found out that they were at odds with other groups like the Hell's-Angels. Tribal rivalry originates in a blinkered conformity to a given image.

Throughout history, clever bishops, kings, lords, barons and other power seekers have manipulated the masses by realising this rule of conformity. By cultivating a state, church, empire or national image for naive populations under their command, leaders and dictators have easily been able to bypass the individual's right to freedom and personal choice. They push the correct buttons to motivate millions in crusades, wars and invasions. This is the real reason why the freethinking individual is always seen as a threat by the establishment.

The author is the founder of the anti-fundamentalist monitoring organisation - 'Pagan Anti-Defamation Network' (PAN). These words represent but one individual's spiritual quest for liberation from the stifling quicksand of cultural and theological oppression. I must emphasise here that each individual Pagan would offer a different slant on the process. Fortunately this is just how it should be as genuine Paganism is not doctrinal or overtly dogmatic. Like nature, from which its stream originates, the Pagan way is one of many wonders, each as diverse and beautiful as the next.

Chapter 1
THE SUBVERSION OF A RELIGION

The old mediaeval witch stereotype of an elderly crone with a black cat has some connection with fact. Since time immemorial, magically enlightened individuals have used animals as detectors of change in the local and distant environment, for warnings of imminent danger and as indicators of the presence of spiritual entities.

Apart from the pure companionship and unconditional love given by cats and dogs to their keepers, these animals do connect with us on deeper levels. This is why shamans have often had a familiar close to hand.

The cat was once a highly venerated creature as in the case of its association with the ancient Egyptian sun goddess Bast or Bastet who was usually depicted as a woman with a cat's head, though she occasionally took on the guise of an ordinary domesticated cat. Apart from having solar attributes, Bast was a goddess of dancing, musical events and unbridled pleasure. Her temple at Bubastis, south of Pelusium, contained many cats which worshippers held to be incarnations of Bast herself. Bast was an extremely ancient goddess, her worship practiced in the Nile Delta from around 3200 BCE. By the year 950 BCE, her popularity was immense and she was honoured as a national deity.

The solar goddess of Egypt, like many other deities, was later to be subjected to the influence of Rome's mythologists. Bast received the honourable vocative of Diana-Bubastis from the time when certain Roman gods were said to have fled into Egypt to escape the wrath of Typhon. Diana was reckoned to have turned herself into the image of a cat. The Roman goddess Diana holds a similar position to Egypt's Bast though Diana, unlike Bast, is frequently associated with the moon; her feline metamorphosis links her with the lunar cycle as the cat has long been associated with night, magic and the moon.

Diodorus, the Sicilian historian, made a great study of Egypt. Although he was often criticised for his lack of attention to detail concerning very important events, he mentioned the summary execution of a Roman who had accidentally killed one of Bast's sacred animals in Egypt, showing just how much the cat meant to the citizens.

Though Bast is a cat-deity she was originally represented as a lion-headed goddess that presided over the fertilising power of the sun. The majestic lion has long been regarded as a symbol of gods and goddesses associated with the energy residing in the sun; without the golden sun everything on earth would cease to exist; a truth our ancient forefathers knew well. The magical link between Bast, the sun and the lion is symbolised by that most precious of metals, gold. It is emblematic of spirituality, glory, purity, superiority and the bright illumination that clears the conscious mind through liberation and the realisation of self. Bast's transformation from a proud lion-headed deity to the domestic cat would seem, at first, to be a demotion, but mirrors humankind's evolutionary step from the wild primordial state to cultivated domestication.

Bast was the benevolent aspect of solar power - the force that gives life. As the good goddess of solar power, Bast represents pure clear illumination, the light of day and mental clarity. Like the sun itself she brings order where before only chaos reigned, her golden life-force banishing all fears, doubts and confusions. Because of her beneficent nature, Bast was a deity to approach when one was feeble, old or sick. She restored health, particularly from mental diseases such as depression, anxiety or persistent worries. This is not surprising when we consider just how many people actually suffer from the lack of sunshine in the winter months. Seasonally affective disorder (SAD) gives rise to all the above symptoms and shortage of the sun's rays can also lead to a deficiency in vitamin D which in turn can result in rickets, osteoporosis and other related diseases.

Bast's long association with the feline probably owes quite a lot to the fact that the Nile Delta area had more than its fair share of serpents and cats, being agile hunters, made excellent snake killers. Phonetically the Egyptian hieroglyph for the snake links with the modern letter Z. The serpent's energy is portrayed in this twisted line of force; its essence manifests on the physical plane in an uneasy zigzag fashion, sometimes beneficial, sometimes the reverse.

While Bast is a radiant personification of the sun's positive countenance, there is another lion-headed sun goddess with a more terrible nature. She was called Sekmet or Sekhmet (the Powerful or Terrible One). Sekmet once tried to destroy the race of man when the great god Ra sent her to crush a human rebellion against him. She got so carried away in the carnage that Ra was forced to calm her down with a magical drink containing ale and the juice of pomegranate. In her rage Sekmet drank the liquid, mistaking it for human blood. Soon intoxication sapped her strength, forcing her to end the brutal destruction. When she woke from her drunken stupor, all rage had gone - just like the setting sun.

The power of Sekmet is an ancient characterization of the sun's malignant, destructive aspect. A thirsty desert wanderer out in the fierce, arid heat of the midday sun will soon discover Sekmet's harmful nature. Contemporary Pagan neophytes could perhaps be forgiven for perceiving Sekmet as a goddess to avoid like the plague. Her seemingly unquenchable lust for annihilation is not as it may at first appear. Occasionally one needs to take evasive action to ensure good health or at least restore it. A god or goddess who (like Sekmet) seems much too aggressive by contemporary standards is perfect to assist in the banishment of many illnesses.

This cat-like duality of good or bad, loving companion or vicious killer can be observed in all things. The sun will warm us when we are cold, making the dark Earth bring forth new life: this is positive. Solar power can also blind a man and reduce his flesh to bone, reducing good fertile meadows to barren dust. The negative, blighting energy of a god-form can be converted into positive healing activity if the adherent applies enough study and conviction to the task at hand. By joining with the deity we call upon the powers of creation. Paganism sees everything in the universe as having its own soul, essence or spirit that dwells within. Every aspect of creation is interconnected; every level of reality works in harmony with all the rest. For example, one cannot move a finger muscle on the physical plane without first formulating this action on the mental level. Every function or skill can be traced back to deeper levels of the particular process involved, eventually cumulating in the highest aspect of spirituality, which Pagans know as the gods. The ancients, in their wisdom, knew this fact very well indeed and because of it developed special magical systems designed to work with the unseen forces in the cosmos.

It is widely believed that the British domesticated cat originated in Egypt, being imported first into Greece then later Italy and finally brought Britain by the Romans. Naturally, some species such as the tabby probably interbred with the native wild cat (*Felis catus*) of the Scottish districts but the Egyptian connection seems to remain quite clear and distinct.

Freya's Cats
The Norse goddess of love, sexuality, magic and the moon was Freya or Freyja, which means 'Lady'. In medieval times any lady of good standing and wealth was referred to as 'Frau' or 'Frouwa' from Freya. Freya gives her name to Friday and she equates with the Roman goddess of love, Venus.

Freya was also known as Gefjon, Horn, Mardoll, Menglod, Syr and Vanadis. Her image occasionally becomes mingled with Frigga or Frigg who was the mother of Balder by Odin. It seems highly likely that Freya and Frigga were originally the same deity, their apparent differences creeping in later as regional divisions forced each competing tribal unit to extend and modify the deity to suit their own growing needs. [a]

Freya was usually depicted as riding through the sky in a chariot drawn by two cats. She was married to Odr (an aspect of Odin). Once, Odr left Freya to venture forth into the realm of mankind. She was so distraught by his loss that she wept tears of shining amber. The deep love and understanding that our forefathers had for their environment is quite clear in the telling of such myths as this; anyone who has ever felt lifted with an inner sense of joy while gazing at golden rain falling on a field of barley in late summer will no doubt feel a certain empathy with Freya's tears.

Freya's popularity was immense, particularly in Sweden. In fact she was the only Scandinavian deity to be placed in the midst of the stars; the Swedish people referred to Orion's Belt as 'Frigga's (Freya's) Distaff'.

In numerous regions of Scandinavia, Freya was associated with the arts of shamanism, magic and the underworld. She was also adept at metamorphosing into the shape of various creatures at will.

The Witch's Cat

The sacredness of one particular religion's symbols and totems frequently becomes a profanity to a conquering faith. The humble cat was to suffer this fate at the hands of the early Christian Church. The pre-medieval Church soon managed to associate Freya's feline steeds with evil and general debauchery. The cat was Freya's animal - the goddess was Pagan so the creature was naturally assumed to be in league with the Devil. During the medieval period cats were no longer seen as creatures of devotion. On the contrary, they were regarded by the early Church as being witches' familiars. In many places throughout Europe, cats (and other pitiable animals) were frequently used as substitutes and cruelly burnt alive by the pious doing 'God's work' in the absence of a human scapegoat.

Such barbaric practices against innocent animals persist even today. In many parts of Spain, old church festival traditions involve the torture and death of cats, bulls, geese, goats and other helpless victims of ecclesiastical superstition. In order to understand precisely why the cat has been given such a hard time throughout the Christian epoch we need to examine the early Christian suppression of native British belief systems.

Witchprickers

The early Church used Pagan myths, like that of Freya, in the most obscene and vile manner. Sadistic witch-finders like Matthew Hopkins (whose reign of terror took place during the English Civil War, especially during the period of 1644-1646) were to use methods of interrogation allied to the Church related view of evil being linked to native Pagan faiths. Any old person, particularly a solitary female, was viewed with suspicion, especially if they showed too much affection to a pet. Such a creature could be regarded as a familiar rendering the owner vulnerable to possible arrest and summary interrogation by witch-finders.

Cats, dogs and many other creatures were believed to suckle at the breasts of witches; the devil would transform himself into an animal then the witch let the beast drink her milk from a secret third nipple. Because of this sort of superstition and ignorance, thousands of innocent men and woman were subjected to the most horrible and humiliating tortures. Witch-finders became witch-prickers; suspects would often be displayed chained and naked in public areas like the market place.

The pricker would then delight in seeking out the victim's additional nipple with a sharp bodkin. [b]

Sometimes the 'sign of the Devil' was believed to take the shape of a birthmark, frequently located near the anus, vagina, tongue, eye or other sensitive private part of the hapless defendant. According to leading demonologists of the day, this Satan's-seal (*Sigillum-diaboli*) occasionally took the likeness of an animal such as a dog, hare, toad, frog, bat or mouse. Often the mark was thought to be insensitive to pain. The pricker, eager to prove his prisoner's guilt, would declare that he had found it using a false bodkin with a retractable point similar to a modern stage actor's fake knife. '*Look, the evil old hag feels no pain*', the inquisitor might shout to the baying crowd. "*Tis the mark of Satan for sure, the witch is found amongst God's good people.*' Being different, non-conformist, solitary, too wise or simply the owner of a friendly cat could be very dangerous during the Burning Times.

During the time of its infancy in Pagan lands, the Church didn't have either the political support or the backing of native Pagans to enforce a total theocratical monopoly. However, gradually changes began to filter through. Laws were created as early as 901 CE (during the reign of Edward the Elder, 900-924) to inflict banishment on those sorcerers practicing divination and associated magical arts. Athalstan (King of the Mercians and West Saxons) declared witchcraft a capital offence in 940. Athelstan's influence was wide, not only over Britain but the whole of Christendom. His many sisters were married off to various continental rulers making alliances throughout Europe, most notably by the marriage of Edhild and Hugh, Count of Paris. Many of the later mediaeval witchcraft persecutions began in European locations, so we may be observing here the very first seeds of a more 'general' intolerance toward unorthodox minorities in the evolving social structure of the day.

The Black Death

The fourteenth century brought with it the horrors of the Black Death or 'Great Pestilence'. It is estimated that approximately 100,000 people perished in London alone following just one visitation of the plague. Conservative studies reckon that between 3,000,000 to 5,000,000 (one third to one half of the total population of Britian) died. In China 13,000,000 died while an estimated 24,000,000 perished throughout the East as a whole. Some reporters of the time speculated that flood, earthquake, famine, drought, dense fog or other natural disasters frequently preceded plague. Strangely, the very seasons themselves were regarded as suffering from a sort of divine sickness. Plague affected the roots of society - bodily illness was severe, but disease of the soul had more far-reaching ramifications. Following the wane of the pestilence, men's minds turned towards finding a reason for all the years of misery and destruction.

Religious fanaticism set in and the Christian moralisers of the period found scapegoats in religious minorities which had previously remained largely ignored. Any individual or group that failed to adhere to the strict doctrine of the Holy Mother Church was suspected of heresy and subject to arrest, torture and possible execution, including unorthodox Christian sects.

Even before the Black Death claimed its first victim, orders like the Templars (a military sect that originated around the time of the Crusades), had felt the wrath of Church and State. The Templar creed was one of extreme courage. 'Glory in battle' and 'never play the coward' were their watchwords; they were wealthy, brave, proud and stubborn. False accusations of indecency, blasphemy and other debaucheries were persistently levelled against the Templars. On the Continent many of these bold knights were racked, burned and forced into giving false confessions against their comrades. Many of them refused to tell lies, and in France on 12th of May 1310 the Church slowly roasted to death fifty-four Templars. The victims, honourable to the last breath, refused to give bogus statements to their inquisitors. In England trials of the Templars were at first conducted with less cruelty. However, direct pressure from the Pope led to the use of hideous tortures.

Judaism didn't escape persecution either. Christian religious intolerance spilled over at Mayence where an estimated 12,000 Jewish people were put to death for being heretics.

Witches had a very nasty time in seventeenth century England. Incarceration was quickly followed by interrogation. It is extremely important for all members of contemporary society (especially modern Pagans and witches) to understand just how and why the witch-hunt hysteria started in the first place.

Propaganda

Today, much of what people regard as hard fact concerning the Burning Times is without doubt early ecclesiastical propaganda. In those days the Church controlled printing; all aspects of ancient indigenous fertility religions had to be suppressed and the printing press gave the Church just the weapon it needed.

This process really started in earnest with two German Dominican monks, Jakob Sprenger and Heinrich (Institor) Kramer. Encouraged by the anti-occultist encyclical *'Summis Desiderantes Affectibus'*, issued by Pope Innocent VIII in 1484, they set about producing their own infamous document *'Malleus Maleficarum'* or 'The Witch-Hammer' (1486-9). The monks first took this to the directors of the theology department at Cologne University where the majority of erudite academics dismissed the effort as wholly unsatisfactory. Not to be deterred, the duo somehow managed to gain the blessing of the college tutors, a forgery not uncovered until the late Victorian era - long after the damage was done.

The *Malleus Maleficarum* was a nadir in the annals of man's inhumanity to man. It contained everything the would-be torturer could ever need to destroy witches. Perceived witches were not now tormented and killed in small groups: they were executed in dozens and hundreds. At Bamberg 600 died in just three months, in Geneva 500 went to the flames in 1515, in Wurzburg 900, at Toulouse 400 were killed in one season, at Lorraine 900. Some prominent authorities have given conservative estimates for the Church's holocaust on Pagans as taking up to 9,000,000 victims. Apologists have sought to play down the estimates for obvious reasons, and hint at death figures in the low thousands. Figures are quite complicated, yet a maximum estimate of 13,000,000 dead and a minimum approximation of 4,000,000 dead are probably as good as we are going to get. The witch mania lasted for centuries.

Free-thinking individuals (especially Pagans) today wonder if contemporary Christian moralisers will ever really admit to their forebears' true guilt in the mediaeval atrocities. Will they ever give the long overdue apology to *all* religious minorities, instead of beatifying, celebrating and generally honouring the evil criminals involved? Sadly if history is anything to go by, today's Pagans will have to wait until Hell freezes over.[c]

These home-truths concerning the criminal deeds by yesteryears' clergy may be very hard for many Christians to stomach. The historical evidence is crystal clear. By elevating the clerics of mediaeval Britain and Europe to sainthood they are doing nothing more than honouring murderers. Every lie told about the ancient Earth-related faith of witchcraft was originally gained through torture. Inquisitors would formulate the questions and the answers required before the victim even set foot into the torture chamber and it was only a matter of time before the rack, thumbscrew or iron-boot forced the poor half-demented woman to admit any crazy thing at all just to stop her pain. The final word on this corruption I shall leave with a man not renowned for his compassion. Sir George Mackenzie sensibly said of Witchcraft:

'Most of these poor creatures are tortured by their keepers, who being persuaded they do God good service, think it their duty to vex and torment their prisoners and I know that most of all that ever were taken were tormented after this manner and this usage was the ground for all their confession'. [d]

The lessons of man's intolerance to his neighbours must never be forgotten lest the fires of hatred once again smoulder and ignite.

The Law Makers
The word 'witch' seems to come from a root which also gives us the old English *wicca* and *witan*. The Witan were a counsel of wise men who gave advice to the monarch before he decided on any important course of action. Even Christian rulers like Alfred (849-900) would never dream of passing laws without their recommendations and always placed new proposals before the Witan. [e]

Similarly, the ancient Pagan Celts had their own wise counsels, the Druids. No level-headed Celtic king or chieftain would go to war, embark on an epic journey or consider peaceful negotiations with a rival tribe without first consulting with his resident druidic advisors.

The Romans also had their wise-counsel, the *Sena'tus* (Senate). Romulus, the legendary founder of Rome, was believed to have inaugurated the Senate to rule the city in his absence. The Senate was, among other things, the upholder of religion; they frequently held assemblies in the temples of Apollo, Jupiter and Concordia etc. Such was the influence of this wise-counsel that it survived for 1,300 years until its abolition in the time of Justinian. The Celtic Britons[f] largely amalgamated their traditions, practices, customs and laws with the Roman ways. This is not surprising when we consider just how long the legions stayed in Britain from Caesar's first landing 55 BCE to Honorius's-departure in 410 CE.

The Germanic law-making machine was a more compact affair than the Romano-British system. It was based on strong loyalty to family and tribal-leader rather than to a whole country, state or empire. The Saxons, Angles, Jutes and other tribes that poured into Britain after the Roman departure brought with them their own brand of wise-counsel. They had, to a greater extent, been insulated from the laws and practices of the Roman Empire; their main contact with Rome was either through merchant trading posts or at the sharp end of a centurion's *gladius* during times of war. The Germanic tribes gave strong allegiance to their *Heretoga* (war-leader); he was protected with a fierce loyalty that ensured each warrior would give his all in battle. Like the Eastern Samurai, death before dishonour was their highest ideal. To die bravely in skirmish with one's chieftain was seen as a great personal achievement. The Angle and Saxon raiding parties referred to their lord as *Hlaford*, meaning 'loaf-giver' because they believed that their very existence rested in his hands. The *Heretoga* frequently became the king, and he usually claimed to have been descended from the sky and wind god, Woden (Odin).

The Wise-Ones
Originally, the Wise-Ones in tribal society were those odd individuals who displayed a certain mystical talent for divining the future, healing the sick and generally seeing to the spiritual needs of the war-leader and his entourage. After their departure, the Romans left their laws and practices in the capable hands of the Celtic peoples.

There had been many revolts by the Celts, the most notable being the Icenian revolution instigated by Queen Boudicca in 60 CE and the Brigantian attack on the Ninth Legion at Eboracum (York) in 120 CE.

The shamanic practices of the druidic priests had been stamped out in many places, probably because the Romans realised that the fierce independence of these holy men often threatened rebellion against imperial authority. With the proclamation of Constantine the Great as the first Christian emperor in Eboracum (306 CE), the Druids, with their Pagan beliefs, were to be suppressed even further. The old earth-orientated ways of the gods of nature were to be pushed deeper and deeper underground.

In the very same year that the semi-Christian Constantine was taking power, the Church was subtly formulating a plan to link all Pagan religious practices with devil-worship. Eight years later in 314 CE, the Council of Ancyra outlawed the practices of witchcraft, sorcery and magic as a method of healing. The penalty for being caught curing the sick through charms or herbal lore was imprisonment. This harsh law forced the native Pagan peoples to give up the wise-ways of their ancestors and countless centuries of hard-earned mystical wisdom.

Later still, King Canute imposed banishment (or in some cases the death sentence) for what he perceived as evil witchery. Canute's reign is often portrayed as one of great law, order and fair policy. This may be true in many ways. However, he punished religious offenders as severely as civil infringers, so his rule was bad news for Pagans at the time. Any person foolish enough to labour on the Lord's Day or be discovered using native charms and spells to heal a sick friend risked invoking just as much anger from Canute as they would have by committing a very serious robbery or crime of violence.

Much of the old magical knowledge didn't just fade away; on the contrary it held fast by passing right back into the hands of the common people. Under differing names, the Old-Craft survived, much to the annoyance of the early Church. The subsequent English Witan aimed to take native shamanic power from the laypeople and, in effect, give them to those in high places. Modern Parliament and Church are the latest resting places for what was once the indigenous birthright of every British man and woman. Today, the official Church stance of frowning on neo-Paganism and all occult beliefs proves, beyond doubt, just how terrified the ecclesiastical machine is of losing its strangle-hold on this nation's spirituality.

The old tribal Saxon and Celtic loyalty to kin is still here with us today, exemplified in the love, honour and respect many people display for their families and friends. In a more negative way, war-band loyalty materialises in the rowdy, misplaced behaviour exhibited by a small minority of soccer hooligans. At the end of the day, it all boils down to the level of spiritual maturity possessed by individuals and groups; such is the complex way of human development and growth.

During the Dark Ages and well into the mediaeval times, country folk living far away from the main centres of population would seek out the solitary village wise-woman or man for assistance with urgent problems of love, health, finance, marriage or family disputes. Such wise-ones would help and heal with cunning herbal lore, wise-counsel, magical knowledge, divination and ancient spells that had been passed down through many generations. Wise men and women were popular with the common people simply because their magic worked - if it hadn't their position would have been untenable.

It would seem feasible to assume that our modern term for a wise-person (witch) comes from the old English and Saxon word 'Witan.' The term *wicca* is masculine, while *wicce* is feminine. We use our wits to think and to know, for without them we do not survive. Other old Anglo-Saxon words that connect with this are *wisian* (lead, guide, show or direct), *wisfaest* (wise), *Wita/Witenagemot* (wise-council or wise man) and *witig* (wise).

Fundamentalism and Christianity
We see what effect fanaticism can have on a culture when we recall the atrocities of the Crusaders under King Richard or the horrors of the Inquisition and Burning Times. More recently we have witnessed the terror attack on the Twin Towers and the controversial counter-actions implemented by western leaders against Iraq and other countries. Fundamentalism enforced by any means is anti-human, unjustifiable and destined to create death, misery and destruction. Any faith may descend into dangerous fundamentalism and as Christianity has influenced western culture so profoundly, let us examine this particular religious path in greater depth and more specifically its historical foundation.

Throughout history, fundamentalists have based their religious dogmatism on nothing but blind uncompromising faith, older rehashed Pagan myths and doctrinal falsehoods. Fundamentalists claim that the historical reliability of the gospels is well established and beyond question. This is certainly not the case. Accounts used by most latter-day fundamentalists come from the four canonical gospels of the Bible. These gospels did not come into the Bible as original and dependable sources from the authors themselves, but from the authority of early Church fathers with political motives. We do not know who actually wrote the gospels, but certainly none of them were written during the alleged lifetime of Jesus. Furthermore, none of the original gospel manuscripts exist today - we only have copies of copies - which make claims for authenticity highly questionable. The Church has described the gospel authors as the apostles Matthew, Mark, Luke and John, but a prominent academic now states, from critical textual investigation, that there is no evidence that the writers could have served as apostles. [g] Today, charismatic clergy still wrongly describe these authors as the genuine disciples of their religion's messiah. This is completely misleading and erroneous in the extreme.

The narratives of the gospels are written in the third person. A genuine observer of events would naturally write in the first person. The Gospel of John deviates from described events in Luke, Mark and Matthew. Moreover, Matthew's writer had evidently gained his information from Mark's gospel. He fashioned his narrative to appeal and fit in with Jewish scriptural tradition. He enhanced the content of Mark's gospel, corrected what he believed to be theologically significant and extended the claimed miracles and supernatural elements. The writer of Luke's gospel acknowledges he is an interpreter of previous literature and not a person giving an eyewitness account; modern academics have indicated that the author of Luke was likely to have been a gentile, or possibly even a Jewish woman. [h]

Another vital point mentioned by serious researchers is that several recorded statements of Jesus were made while he was said to be alone. [i] Who exactly heard what he was supposed to have said? This becomes even more perplexing when the gospel writers record what Jesus actually thought about.

Undoubtedly, the gospels utilize techniques that fiction writers still use to this day. The gospel authors were Jews writing within the *midrashic* tradition and intended their stories to be read as interpretive narratives, not historical accounts. Researchers claim that the gospels can only be hearsay at best and at worst tales created by leading zealots of the day for their own ends. Remember that *New Testament* writings were created after the assumed death of Jesus by unidentified authors and no original *New Testament* documents exist today. [j]

"Yet today, there are few Biblical scholars-- from liberal sceptics to conservative evangelicals- who believe that Matthew, Mark, Luke, and John actually wrote the Gospels. Nowhere do the writers of the texts identify themselves by name or claim unambiguously to have known or travelled with Jesus." [k]

All the denunciation by the early Church of Pagan aspects within their religion is nothing more than hypocritical pretence. Christian theology was originally based on transforming the Jesus figure into yet another fertility, death and resurrection god - another Tammuz, Attis, Adonis, Dionysus or Osiris, each marked by an annual death and renewal which symbolizes the Earth's natural fertilisation and the spiritual renewal within each of us. The Church saw how attractive such ancient Pagan concepts were to the masses and adopted them for their own ends.

This stratagem led to a corruption of the original, wholesome Pagan concepts. Polytheistic and pantheistic philosophy is largely tolerant and well able to adopt other deities, customs and traditions into its cosmology. For instance, the Romans amalgamated many of their deities and traditions with the native Celtic pantheon and even set up shrines to both sets of gods and goddesses. Conversely, monotheistic philosophy is exclusive and intolerant. At base doctrinal level, it states that its revelation of the godhead is the only acceptable way to salvation and that all other faiths are corrupt, bogus or in league with Satan. Understandably, the more liberal-minded have tried to minimize the effects of these bigoted aspects in their religion, yet the leaders resort to the fundamental and elitist core of their credo as and when times demand. How many wars has the chant *'our God reigns'* caused throughout history?

Pantheistic and monotheistic cosmologies are polarised world-views. The forces of monotheism have long declared their sacred duty is to make every living person on the globe one of their own for their own good. Such hard-line missionary aims are anathema to Pagan concept and practice.

Hijacking Pagan Beliefs

We can now observe how more aspects from Paganism were hijacked by the early Church; critical features that show how fundamentalism usurps traditional Pagan myths, symbols and customs:

- The Egyptian goddess Neith was a virgin mother.
- The goddess Isis gave birth, as a virgin, to the god Horus.
- Attis was son of the virgin Nana. His birth was celebrated on 25th December.
- The Roman saviour Quirrnus was born of a virgin.
- Adonis/ Tammuz was born of the virgin Myrrha.
- Mithra/ Mithras was born of a virgin (on 25th December).
- Zoroaster was born of a virgin.
- Krishna was born of a virgin
- Buddha was born of the virgin Maya.
- Indra was born of a virgin.

These are but a few examples which show that the concept of virgin birth is absolutely nothing new. Ancient images of Isis and child predate the Christian Madonna and child. Christian apologists are especially quick to shed doubt on such information, yet the facts remain that the Bible and gospel authors incorporated such imagery into their newly emergent theology.

Numerous mythical figures, such as Horus, Bacchus, Hercules, Osiris, Mithra, Hermes, Prometheus and Perseus (and possibly their parallel god-figures from different cultures)

- All lived in a time prior to the Christian messiah
- All had a deity for a parent
- All had a human virgin for a mother
- All had their birth announced by heavenly display
- All were believed to have been born in December (the winter solstice)
- All had an attempt on their life by a despot while they were a baby
- All met with a brutal demise
- All rose again after their death

The unidentified authors of the gospels were so impressed that they utilised this type of Pagan mythology when creating their own accounts, as without it their newly-hatched concept of divinity, Christ, would have failed to live up to the mythological standard which the people demanded.

The Bible was constructed by religious activists. Each new translator gave their own particular biased slant to the earlier literature, and each century saw new additions based on the personal or political whims of the latest rewriters. Editing and construction of the Bible came from fundamentalists within the early Church. Doctrinal authority within the Church possessed the raw text matter and decided exactly what would appear in the Bible. Subsequent to the original being translated into the Latin tongue, it was only a matter of time before the original language could be done away with. During the Middle Ages the death penalty was often applied to any ordinary person caught trying to read the Bible. Church authority had to be preserved at all costs; thus the individual in the street remained no wiser due to enforced ignorance.

Even Christian-orientated historians such as Sir James Fraser concede the deceitfulness of the early Church and confess that the martyrs, saints, traditions and customs of the Christian Church were stolen from ancient Pagan sources. In fact, the whole Christian calendar is blatantly moulded on the earlier Pagan agricultural year. Furthermore, many Christian and secular historians freely admit that events in the New Testament were taken from much earlier Pagan mythology.

The real meaning of divine death and resurrection is the demise and rebirth of nature's cycle each new season. The Church simply substituted this Pagan wisdom by swapping a sun god for a Son-of-God. This was a clever and effective tactic to manipulate people away from their ancient birthright.

It is claimed that there are some two hundred gospels, epistles and other books relating to the Jesus saga. Out of these, only twenty-seven are acknowledged by Church authority. The other one hundred and seventy-three have been declared by the Church to be fraudulent documents and heretical writings.

Dishonesty was apparently quite acceptable. The 4th century Church father and Bishop of Caesarea, Gregory of Nazanzius, wrote to St. Jerome:

'A little jargon is all that is necessary to impose on the people. The less they comprehend, the more they admire.'

Augustine of Hippo, arguably the greatest figure in Christian antiquity, freely wrote:

'It is lawful, then, to him that discusses disputes and preaches of things eternal, or to him that narrates of things temporal pertaining to religion or piety, to conceal at fitting times whatever seems fit to be concealed.'

The 4th century Bishop and ecclesiastical historian, Eusebius, openly bragged that he deceitfully concealed all that would be a disgrace to early Christianity. Too many Church authorities to mention here have followed his early example over the centuries - as they still do today. Eusebius even related, as truth, a preposterous account of directing a letter to Jesus Christ and then receiving a response. If that's not enough to merit serious questioning of his word try this for size. Eusebius claimed

'On some occasions the bodies of martyrs who had been devoured by wild beasts, upon the beasts being strangled, were found alive in their stomachs.'

Unfortunately, a plethora of examples of early Christian deceitfulness abound which simply adds further doubt as to the authenticity behind any contemporary fundamentalist claims. Add to this the fact that ecclesiastical authorities edited and transformed vast swaths of the Bible and you get a picture of the subterfuge residing just under the surface of the fundamentalist mindset.

Following this general pattern of enquiry we must, for the sake of both fairness and precision, also ask if alleged miracles are exclusive to the Jesus myth. Please note that Pagan deities (and real historical persons) were accredited with not only performing a variety of miracles, but miracles identical to those of Jesus, some long before he was said to exist. When the Jewish historian and traitor Josephus described Vespasian, the famous Roman general and emperor, as the 'Messiah', he was referring to an actual human being and real-life proceedings, not a mythological figure. Josephus was shrewd and knew well that by flattering Vespasian he might have had a better chance of survival after his capture by Roman forces.

Doubt must also be cast on Josephus's objectivity as he was meant to have taken the honourable way out, committing suicide with all his Jewish comrades, after the siege of Jotapata in 67 CE. Somehow Josephus survived this and was then taken to Vespasian. He predicted that Vespasian would become the ruler of the 'entire world'. Josephus threw in his lot with the Romans and was rewarded for his efforts but branded a collaborator by the Jews. In light of this, it is rather difficult to grant proper historical authority to a self-seeking individual who turned against his own people to save his own skin – a person whose words are given by Christian apologists as some sort of firm, unbiased evidence of the genuine historicity of their chosen saviour. It would never stand up in any fair-minded contemporary court of law.

Apart from Josephus's Jesus account, some scholars have had serious doubts about his other writings such as his version of the tragedy at Masada which is apparently contradicted by archaeological evidence.[1] According to Josephus, the killing of the 960 residents of Masada and the obliteration of the palace was the deliberate act of all the people acting in agreement. However, the archaeological remains cannot be reconciled with this account. His writings may be nothing more than interpolations by later proselytising Christian copyists.

It is very illuminating to note that Vespasian was recorded by Tacitus and Suetonius as curing a blind man with his spittle; a messianic figure making the blind see again. Vespasian is also apparently reported to have 'healed the lame'. Does this sound familiar?

Early Christian theologians borrowed heavily from Pagan mythology as the following examples will show:

- Asclepius was the son of Apollo and he reputedly raised the dead and cured the sick.
- The Egyptian goddess Isis healed the sick
- Pythagoras prophesised, healed the sick and calmed storms
- Dionysus changed water into wine
- Poseidon walked on water

Countless more examples, which antedate Christianity, exist. Before the Christian saga was first created, hundreds of Pagan miracles were believed to have occurred and many were dead ringers for the supernatural tales attributed to Jesus.

It is perhaps worthwhile to briefly focus on one god in particular, Mithras, who almost overthrew the growing Christian Church and whose traditional rites, festivals and customs were later incorporated into Christianity. Remember that the story of Mithra precedes the Christian myth by approximately six-hundred years.

Mithras was exceedingly popular with the Roman legions. His name stems from the Indo-Iranian god Mitra or Mithra. Mithra was believed to have been born of a virgin on December 25th. His birthday was adopted by Christians in the

4th century as the birthday of Christ. He was considered to be a travelling tutor and master. Mithra's nativity was witnessed by Magi and shepherds who brought gifts to his birth-cave. He had twelve companions or disciples. His religion had a Eucharist or 'Lord's Supper.' Mithra also had a major resurrection festival, which later become Easter. His followers knew him amongst other things as 'the Good Shepherd,' 'The Way, the Truth and the Light', 'the Redeemer', 'the Saviour' and 'The Messiah.' Prior to his return to heaven, Mithra held a Last Supper with his twelve disciples, who represented the signs of the zodiac. In remembrance of this event, his followers partook of sacramental bread (Holy Communion) marked with a cross. He was believed to have performed miracles and after being buried in a tomb he rose again after three days. He was identified with both the lamb and the lion and his holy day was Sunday - The Lord's Day. The Mithraic feast day of the Epiphany, which heralded the arrival of the sun-priests 'Magi,' was later adopted by the Christian Church.

Recall that this entire occurrence was centuries previous to the manifestation of the Christ legend. Everything that the Church has professed to be its own is undoubtedly nothing of the sort. Original thinking was not then a great criterion for the Christian Church fathers who, as we can see, adopted virtually everything from earlier Pagan culture and tradition.

So what about any crucified gods before the Jesus tale? In ancient times it was supposed that execution by crucifixion caused the highest extreme of suffering possible, therefore, a divine being undergoing such misery was a model of bravery and courage. The god must be greater than his subjects to be able to suffer the most horrible method of death without complaint. Here are a few examples to consider:

- Ixion: a Thessalian sun god, know as 'the crucified spirit of the world.' He was said to have borne the sins of the world on his back.
- The god Bali of Orissa: crucified 725 BCE - also known as Bel.
- Mithra of Persia: crucified, 600 BCE.
- Crite of Chaldea: crucified, 1200 BCE
- Thammuz and Dumuzi and Adonis of Syria: crucified 1160 BCE
- Wittoba of the Telingonesic: crucified 552 BCE
- Iao of Nepaul: known as 'the crucified saviour' crucified 622 BCE
- Hesus of the Celtic Druids: crucified 834 BCE
- Quexalcote of Mexico: crucified (between two thieves) 'for the sins of mankind' 587 BCE
- Quirinus of Rome: crucified 506 BCE
- Prometheus: crucified 547 BCE
- Crucifixion of Thulis of Egypt, 1700 BCE

- Indra of Tibet: crucified 725 BCE
- Alcestos of Euripides (female deity): crucified 600 BCE
- Atys of Phrygia: by some accounts crucified 1170 BCE
- Furthermore, Osiris was allegedly crucified in the heavens by some accounts, as was Horus.

Many of those above figures had identical themes in their respective tales to the Christ legend, which they predated by centuries. Fundamentalists within the early Church naturally wanted to keep the monopoly on this divine concept so they used every available effort to conceal from public knowledge the fact that they had extracted this literature from Pagan mythology.

Sadly, monotheistic deception has twisted once wholesome native Pagan polytheistic traditions, which linked man with the universal cycles of the earth, moon, sun and stars, into something that they never were. The beautiful, edifying ancient Pagan myths created by our ancestors were originally well-judged analogies for essential seasonal events and were never meant to be corrupted into man-made fantasies that give power to priesthoods in positions of high authority.

Paganism Got There First

Fundamentalist apologists have sought to defend their corner by suggesting that Pagan legends may have been based on stories from the *Old Testament* but, as we have already seen, the biblical texts have been so utterly contaminated throughout time that such a presumption certainly would never stand up in a court of law. Even if this Christian claim were true, where exactly do the apologists think the *Old Testament* writers got their ideas from? Are these apologists actually trying to modify archaeological evidence and historical fact?

Apart from the Mithraic legend's great similarities to the newer Jesus fable, as we have observed, numerous resurrection/ crucifixion/ virgin birth tales from various places across the globe have been celebrated by many different cultures and long before the first Christian mythologists started creating their rewrites of this much older Pagan prose. It is impossible to know the exact dates and precise timing of a particular myth's source, yet unlike monotheistic man-made credo, Pagan myths have been handed down since time immemorial – ever since mans' first attempt to communicate with the life-essence of the planet. Many Pagan cultures which existed thousands of miles apart and could never have communicated had similar legends in common.

Possibly the most ridiculous ingredient in the apologetics' pie is that the *Old Testament* was written by Jews who shunned Paganism. Whoever the writers were (Jews or otherwise) they would doubtless have been influenced by eons of inherited Pagan myths handed down to them from innumerable preceding generations.

Generally, scholars concur that the *Old Testament* was compiled between the 12th and the 2nd century BCE. However, in relative terms of mythological time scale, this *Old Testament* phase seems rather insignificant.

Chapter 2
THE GODS

Magic is the creative or destructive power of the cosmos. This power manifests on all levels of existence. We humans, as intelligent, self-conscious beings, have the ability to manipulate magical energy. Our consciousness of self gives us the means to become in AT-ONE-MENT (atonement) with every other person, animal, tree, rock, river etc. in this home that we know as Mother Earth.

Many folk will instinctively feel the divine spark of spirituality inherent in nature. A solitary walk by a beautiful river, a stroll through a wood in May, or the awesome thrill of an approaching thunderstorm in late summer - all such natural phenomena can make even the most ordinary, irreligious person hanker for more of those primordial feelings of elation that grow from such experiences. Many years ago such feelings made me want to discover more of the euphoric at-one-ness with 'magical' hidden nature.

As a child I often experienced *deja vu*. Something told me that I had been to certain unknown places before. I didn't just believe this; I actually knew. I also had experiences of flights over rooftops and fields which I later found out to be occurrences of what some folk were calling astral projection. I discovered the beauty of spirit in a frosty spider's web, a green nettle-patch, a shoal of sticklebacks darting in a babbling brook; in fact I found it in every aspect of the natural world that I was exposed to. Today I have rediscovered magical nature anew with Pagan ritual in its many forms.

Recently I found out from my mother that my grandmother and my great grandmother were very popular in their day with friends and neighbours. They consulted the cards, tea leaves and crystal ball for friends and family, being in much demand. Maybe occult interest has been passed down to me from ancestors of old on some sort of genetic-memory level, or could my love of the hidden world be something that has always been with me through many reincarnations? Romantic fancy or not, I like to think (and my gut feeling tells me) that it's true. I found that in order to grow spiritually, I had first to eradicate the monotheistic brain-washing that had been drummed into me from childhood. A detailed study of native Pagan mythology was the tonic needed to counter my indoctrination. I discovered that all Christian feast days were based on much older Pagan festivals. I also discovered that Jesus Christ was not by any means the first sun-god figure. Adonis, Attis, Osiris and many others got there first. So what was all this blarney about the one true faith and resurrection all about then? The Christians had hijacked our birthright. I also realised that magical energy was just waiting to be explored, it was everywhere around me in the trees, hills and fields. It had been there all along, so why lock it away in some stuffy old man-made place of worship like a church?

We need names to understand (at a ground level) the aspects of human experience and consciousness that work through, in and around us, so we call them gods or spirits. These personifications of our world are real if we open up our true selves to them. It's useless to just give them lip-service as many Neo-Pagans do. We must raise up our minds and souls to the gods. We have to give to them in order to link with them if we truly want to journey into greater wisdom, awareness and spiritual growth. It is the sacrifice of the old-self that propels us forward; Mithras slaying the Sun-Bull (his own negative self) illustrates this point admirably. Incidentally, many legends and myths share the theme of the sacrifice of the god's old self to rise again, reborn anew, the Christian deity just being the most recent addition to the original list.

The God-Forms

The god-forms used in magical ritual are dependent on the psychological and cultural make-up of the individual witch and magician concerned. Many practitioners seem to need the security of what they see as an established structure with maybe a Celtic (Druidic) or Norse (Odinic) pantheon of deities. Some prefer to be more exotic with Voodoo, Japanese or Oceanic gods. This matters not so long as one is comfortable working with a given pantheon of deities.

I work largely with the Roman gods simply because I find that the blend of complex classical imagery and native sense of belonging suits my personality very well. After all, much of this country's spiritual heritage is owed to the Roman Pagan influence. They merged their gods with Celtic deities and 'improved' upon them. The Romans anthropomorphized ideal and perfect human concepts such as love, maternity, courage and joy in the images of the gods; this ensured that every individual could relate to the ideal being sought. Such strong personification of divinity marked a radical change in British culture. To actually see representations of the gods was to know them on a more intimate level. This enabled worshippers to reach much greater levels of awareness of themselves and the world.

The Romans had gods and goddesses for everything in creation and that suits me extremely well too. In Roman belief, it wasn't only the sky, earth or water that had its own inherent spirit, as in more primitive societies. Actions, concepts and bland everyday things such as doors, gardens, sowing, wine, humour and stimulation had their own deity. This I find a greatly acceptable, beautifully pure and spiritual concept. The fact that the pragmatic Romans gave everything and its action its own presiding deity compliments present day magical (and even scientific) theory very nicely indeed. Everything vibrates at differing frequencies and rates and has its own particular aura, signature of essence and electro-magnetic energy field and so on; in other words, its own god and spirit-force. This lets you explore spirituality in everyday life and in every place.

Early man, with his limited capacity for understanding, sought to join with the many forces that affected his world. This was a tremendously important step in the early development of our species. Our first experiences of religious growth were essentially shamanic or magical and these first tentative steps have never been superseded. Contemporary men and women have a great urge to return to the basic shamanic roots of our ancestors.

The doorway to the gods is unlocked with a different key by each individual who seeks their own truth. All spiritual paths, figuratively speaking, lead us to Rome, ergo we can use Rome as a symbolic metaphor marking man's spiritual quest towards divine grace, and will further explore this later.

The Fairies

Before we leave the subject of the gods, we must consider one significant topic which is the source of much misunderstanding, and that is the realm of fairy lore. What are we to make of the winged, ephemeral creatures that inhabit the hidden regions of the human mind and the overgrown forests where our ancestors once worshipped the Old Gods?

When the first Celts came to these isles around 600 years before Caesar's legions marched in, they brought with them their own brand of polytheistic religion. Each mountain, stone, tree, lake, hill and river was seen as having its own tutelary deity. This concept is not only peculiar to the Gaelic or Brythonic Celts, other Pagan races viewed the world in a comparable manner. The Romans believed that everything and its action contained a spiritual entity, the *genius-loci* and the spirit within. The personal *genius* of a man possessed two aspects, one positive and the other negative. When these existed in harmony, balance was achieved. If, however, the genius was discontented, then mental destruction was imminent.[m] These companions influenced a man's destiny by their respective good and bad behaviour. *Genialis* guarded over the affairs of the marriage bed, the place of generative reproduction, giving rise to the modern words 'generative', 'genital' and 'generation'. *Genii* protected men from the moment of their birth, while women were guarded by the *Junones*.[n]

The fact that many gods and goddesses were seen as being winged (e.g. Cupido and Cupid, Victoria and Victory) gives us a clue to their later transformation into fairies. When the first Christian missionaries arrived in Britain, they embarked upon a holy mission to entice the indigenous people away from their Earth-orientated beliefs. Long worshipped deities were demoted into lesser beings. Some were changed into holy saints, like the Celtic fire goddess Brighid who ended up being canonized as Saint Brigit of Kildare. Horned-gods of nature and fertility such as Pan and Herne were equated with Satan, whilst other deities ended up as heroic kings and elegant queens. and others became fairies.[o]

Fairy-hills abound in these isles where great deities once held the loyalty and love of the honest country folk. If we bother to trace it, the wailing cry of the Banshee ('Woman of the Hill') will lead us back to various aspects of the Gaelic goddess of war, Badbh. Finvarra, the king of the Irish fairies, is the modern counterpart of a powerful Irish deity who once presided over wine cellars and stables. After the defeat of the Tuatha De Danann at the hands of the Milesians, Finvarra was assigned the *Sidh Meadha* (an underground dwelling at Knockma). Many other deities were also given subterranean realms by the earth god Dagda at various locations throughout Ireland. Naturally, with time and the push of monotheism, the Old Gods came to be seen as somewhat inferior beings, the fairy-folk of legend. This subtle demotion of native divinities can be traced in practically all countries. In fact, wherever we find evidence of ancient traditions and customs involving pixies, fairies, trolls, elves or other beings of the mystical unseen world, we discover evidence of the suppression of original Pagan faiths. Try as it may, the Church has been quite incapable of completely eradicating native spirituality from the hearts and minds of the common people. Our fairy lore is a vital and distinct link to the essential, religious aspects of our pre-Christian heritage.

Another school of thought suggests that fairy lore originates from the ancient race-memory we possess of earlier civilisations. Aboriginal Stone Age tribes hunted and farmed these lands long before the earliest Celts arrived. Ancient monuments of stone covered the landscape and the Celts' trepidation on first seeing these must have been enormous. The Neolithic inhabitants were neither uncivilised nor stupid; they had their own richly unique culture and the Celts no doubt quickly discovered this fact.[p] These ancient stone-using peoples were eventually overtaken and amalgamated, but never quite removed by the technically superior metal-crafting Celts.

These Neolithic people must have seemed quite strange to the Celts, their customs and traditions being markedly different in many ways. The Celts must certainly have feared and yet respected them, not because of their size or weaponry but because, like all conquering races, they knew very little of the magical ways of their opponents. The Roman Legionaries found themselves in a similar uncomfortable position of awed apprehension when they faced their first screaming, woad-painted Celtic charioteers and the wild druidic priests who stood in their way.

In popular folklore the fairies are afraid of iron. It is also believed that they have tribes, families and weddings, live in caverns and have a magical ability to control the weather. Is this not perhaps proof of an older, largely unknown culture? Could this be evidence of the ancient Celtic dread of an old primitive (yet deadly) tribal adversary possessing shamanic skills beyond the scope and understanding of the supposedly more advanced Iron Age conquerors?

The above comments seek to explain (albeit briefly) the place of fairies in the 'physical' scheme of things. We can only venture a short distance on the worldly road when exploring fairy lore. We must endeavour to look behind the obvious to find the hidden, mystical language dwelling deep within the land of the fair-people. Magic is the power of creation, it is neither good or bad; it is, like electricity or lightening, merely there. Fairies can be seen as magical creatures that have evolved, like us, within a certain reality. They have been appreciated as entities that dwell on an elemental plane of existence somewhere between man and the gods, living just under or over the physical level, where solid reality has not yet quite managed to achieve full materialisation.

Some have sought to portray them as personifications of the spiritual action which ensures activity in the natural cycle. Just because we cannot always see something does not mean that it does not exist. If we stand in front of a stationary aeroplane's propeller it is visible, filling a given place in space and time. We understand this, it is logical, yet what happens if the propeller is spinning at very high speed? It seems to disappear from view although it is still there. A similar thing occurs when a dog-whistle is blown. The hound zooms in on the call. However, a human cannot hear this high frequency. The reality stands; an event has taken place beyond the normal range of our senses.

Our consciousness is conditioned to accept certain defined data while ignoring much that surrounds us in the everyday world - 'things that go bump in the night'. Things also go bump in the day, yet our mundane consciousness is programmed to ignore these events: we simply block out things that do not interest us most of the time. In a crowded room full of chatting people we can tune-in to one voice yards away at will, even though nobody else seems to hear the same thing. The other voices are there too, but we simply don't allow them to enter into our conscious mind. They are (like the wee good fairy-folk) still there. What we are talking about here is awareness of the universe that surrounds and works through us.

We all possess what is sometimes called a psychic filter or censor. This device protects us from psychic overload. Most of the time, we need to work and function on a mundane level of existence for survival. ⁋ Opening the psychic senses through magical ritual, trance, meditation or divination is a path to greater spiritual awareness. Many people claim to have seen or heard the fairy-folk whilst entranced by the wonder of nature in a cornfield, forest or glen. These encounters may be the creations of the overactive mind, but they may also be the result of a lowering of the psychic filter, allowing experience just out of reach of the everyday human faculties.

Genuine fairy lore is a vital part of our indigenous Pagan culture. We must realise that this is our spiritual birthright. Smell the pine tree's fragrance by light of the full moon, hear the sad call of the solitary moorland curlew, feel the warm southern breeze from the sea and open up your own personal awareness to exciting new possibilities. If you don't, then you are missing much of the universe around you and only living half an existence. The next time you see a picture of a fairy in the high street gift shop, think about your wondrous Pagan heritage that has helped to forge such an image of magical beauty. Celebrate life, celebrate nature and know the blessing of the Old Gods inherent in the realm of the mysterious good-folk.

The Gods in Dreams
The gods come to each person differently. Early man found them through wonderment, desire, greed, hunger, love, hate, sorrow and fear. All states of human-consciousness can and do lead us back to the realm of the gods. This is because the gods are like tuning signals, linking us to the vital wholeness of divinity of which we are a part. The gods talk to us all the time, even in our most mundane daytime-consciousness. All we have to do is *listen*. In dreams, the gods communicate with us via the subconscious mind, showing us many self-truths and the answers to life's problems. Because of this, it is always prudent to train yourself to remember and write down dreams the next morning before they are forgotten.

The conscious mind deals with analytical, logical thinking. The subconscious mind acts as a type of messenger bringing knowledge from the deep unconscious into the light of conscious understanding. It speaks to us in symbols. The dream images we see are magical representations of ideas, concepts and emotions that we must learn to heed in order to stay healthy on all levels. The gods show us what we need to know and to ignore this gift is unwise and leads to the stagnation of spiritual evolution.

Our ancestors evolved into increasingly higher planes of spirituality. Mankind started on the epic, religious and magical quest for knowledge of self and place within the changing order of the cosmos. Strange nocturnal dream-scenes could be shared and discussed with others and the archetypal symbolism of the gods became greater and more widely understood. Powerful archetypal images representing the forces of nature that work within, through and outside of us have been passed down to us from our ancestors.[r] The titanic symbols that the ordinary person encounters in the dreamtime or during periods of emotional need are one method that the gods use to ensure our well being and survival. The ancients realised the gods work through dreams in three distinct ways:

- Firstly in dreams of divination, in which the dreamer sought answers to pressing questions from the gods.

- Secondly, dreams that come as warnings or prophecies whereby the gods warn of dangers, great events to come and so on.
- Finally, dreams that come in a totally unexpected manner where the gods appeal to the dreamer's conscious self to atone for past misdemeanours.

One certain path to unbalance, or even madness, is to ignore the disturbing images of a recurring nightmare. The higher conscious mind, known to some as the super-consciousness or unconscious, is the vehicle that the gods use to originate new concepts, thoughts and ideas within us. During sleep, the mundane-conscious mind rests and ordinary events can sometimes be reflected in our dreams, but dreams are more than strange pictures from the sub-conscious mind - they are manifestations from that deep part of self that connects us to the collective unconscious or World Soul. This universal level contains all knowledge of past history and it forms within our psyches a golden bridge enabling us to connect with the gods.

Today, we often hear people ask, *'are we alone in the universe?'* usually referring to extra-terrestrial life, but on a magical level we have never been alone. Consciousness, the Gods' gift to us, ensures that we coexist and connect with all manifestations of the life-force, on earth and beyond. Consciousness gives us understanding of the Gods and gives the Gods understanding of us. This symbiotic relationship has been evolving ever since the first Palaeolithic man lifted his arms high to honour the life-giving sun.

To strike a blunt analogy, the subconscious mind is like a tame hawk, whilst the consciousness is its trainer. The falconer must keep his eye on the bird at all times or else it may revert to wild behaviour. The hawk must listen to its trainer's whistles and calls, or risk going without food and care. The hunt in this scenario is our quest for personal development, knowledge and understanding of the cosmic forces that surround us. The trained hawk is liable to run into trouble without the guiding hand of its owner.

Meditation

The most important thing the witch must do is to listen to his/her inner self - silence is essential to allow the gods room to speak from within. This is why holy men and mystics have sought the solitude of mountains and other such places. The pressures of modern life - the boss at work, personal relationships, health worries and financial troubles - stop us entering the silence and achieving our full potential. The gods help those individuals who make the sincere effort to find them, whether through solitude, meditation, study or ritual workings. In solitude the mind becomes clearer. In places of tranquillity it becomes more focused. It is in these quiet places that the gods imbue the seeker with new perspectives and opportunities.

Meditation is a method of tuning in to divinity. Meditation allows us to still the restless mind giving the deeper levels space to come through. The practice of meditation links us to the life-force. The calmness of meditation, if experienced on a frequent basis, affects our everyday lives; think of the serenity often seen on the faces of eastern mystics and gurus.

Simple meditation is quite effortless. Many practitioners suggest that meditation should be done at the same time each day. This is wise advice, but the pressures of modern life do not always allow us to do so. Making the effort to meditate whenever possible is what really counts.

Find a comfortable spot where you won't be disturbed. Many witches and occultists prefer to cast a magical circle about themselves before meditating to repel negative energies. This can simply be a matter of visualising a white field of energy surrounding you like a glowing, protective cocoon.

Clothing should be unrestricted. If weather and surroundings allow, then no clothes at all (sky-clad) is to be preferred. Special robes for meditation and magic ritual are now freely available and also very good for this purpose.

Sit on the floor with your back straight, cross-legged or alternatively sit on a chair with a straight back. Some people like to meditate lying down which is fine although falling asleep is always a danger.

Next, you must still the restless mind. This is achieved by directing your consciousness to relax the physical body. First close your eyes. Then, starting at the toes, say to yourself: '*My toes are warm, heavy and relaxed.*' Feel them glowing and calm. Try to think of nothing else but your warm toes. Next tell your feet the same: '*My feet are warm, heavy and relaxed.*' Work right through until you have reached the top of your head. Don't worry if the mind wanders with your early efforts. Practice makes perfect and the conscious mind is like an unruly dog that needs training, so keep at it.

By the time you get to your head the whole body should be relaxed. Once you have shut yourself off from every-day chatter in this way you must project your inner-focus into the deeper, quiet realms of the mind. Do this by focusing on the 'third eye', located slightly above and between the two eyes. See nothing but blueness. If other images come into your blue then just let them drift quietly by and pass on. Do not enter into mental dialogue with them. Be the casual observer of these visions, not an active participant. If you can't visualise blue don't worry just stick with the colour that you can see. Some people get white, green or pink more easily and that's just fine too. What we really require is a blank astral space that some people perceive as sky or sea.

A lot of meditators will settle at this stage for the tranquil no-mind state that is now felt. This can be held for ever greater lengths of time with practice. Any strong images that are visualised should be (like dreams) analysed later on when normal consciousness is regained. It is surprising how often one can have revelations and creative ideas following trips into the blue. The gods and energies come into this realm to give us greater knowledge, knowledge that remains mostly inaccessible on material, mundane levels. Dreams and visions are then gifts from the gods sent down to us to inspire, warn us and predict events to come. They also heal us from past harms, jogging us into recalling things that must be remembered for whatever reasons the gods see fit.

Subsequent to the meditation you may feel purer and more attuned with yourself and the universe. It is wise not to rush too quickly out of the meditation; instead you should allocate a brief period for your consciousness to fully reinstate itself before arising. The practical witch or occultist should also keep a diary of any images/symbols that may appear during meditation for later analysis.

There is much wisdom in the numerous books on symbols and dreams, but it must be borne in mind that any one symbolic image can, and frequently does, mean different things to different people. For example, suppose an oak tree crops up in a dream. Popular books on the subject usually give the tree as a symbol meaning growth, stability and success but the standardization of interpretation does not allow for the individual life-experience of the dreamer.

Let's take an example of three people dreaming of an oak tree. Our first dreamer is an old woman who lives alone in an apartment. As a child she would walk for miles in the countryside, playing in the oak woods with her dog. She was safe and happy then; life was fun and carefree. She now looks out through her window into the old gnarled branches of the oak tree and smiles. The rustling leaves bring back the lost beauty of days long past. For her, the oak represents her youth, happiness and golden days of pleasure.

The second candidate is a reluctant tree surgeon who works hard for little money. The work is dirty, physically tiring and dangerous. For him the tree is hard and unyielding. It will take him many hours of gruelling labour to prune back its enormous branches. For him the symbol of the oak means trouble, hardship and risk.

Our last example is a young, female shop assistant. Every night, after work, she waits under the great oak outside her flat, looking impatiently at her wristwatch waiting for her lover's arrival. She paces anxiously, hoping he will come. He's late, he always is, but she smiles at the thought of him as she gazes at the oak. To her the oak is a symbol of patience, longing and love.

The person best qualified to deal with dream and vision interpretation is always the beholder of the vision. Your own private insights into dream and vision are the ones that really matter the most – not mine.

There are however times when the generalisation of symbols does hold true. Ninety-nine people out of one hundred would consider the vision of a man-eating shark biting their leg as being a terrifying image. Alternatively, it would be difficult for most folk to view the vision of a beautiful blue butterfly with anything other than pleasure and wonderment. For this reason I have included a list of symbols in Appendix 4.

Chapter 3
RITUAL

The seeker who has ventured to follow the trail set by this book so far may now be questioning his previous worldview, especially if he comes from a religiously suppressive background. He may rightly state that it is all very well speaking of self-liberation and freedom from oppression, but ask how this can be put into action in everyday life. The answer to this is quite simple, and that answer is *magic*.

The type of magic we are interested in here is the awesome creative force that allows growth and expansion on all planes of existence. Magic can be as simple or as complicated to perform as one wishes. Magic was common to all ancient cultures and still resides deep in the subconscious mind of even the most materialistic western person. This is simply because magic is the quintessential force of individuality which enables us to become greater in every aspect of our lives.

Once a Pagan lifestyle has been seriously considered, then it is preferable to perform some sort of self-initiation rite. This gesture enables the novice to mark the transition from one way of life into another in a sacred manner. It is best to perform the rite just prior to the full moon and, if possible, naked.

Preparing the Sacred Space

A circle surrounds the altar. For the solitary worker, this need be no larger than feels comfortable. It is either painted or marked on the ground with chalk or salt. Alternatively, it can be fashioned from a long piece of cord or rope. The circle marks the boundary between the sacred and the mundane worlds. It holds the power that we raise within and also keeps out what is not required. Whatever sort of circle is used, it should be started and finished in the east, for this is the place that the life-giving sun rises each day.

The altar is situated in the east and a small table will be adequate for our purpose. Drape a single white cloth over it and place a candleholder with a white candle toward the southern direction. Burn initiation incense in a suitable censer, or failing that you can use a dish containing sand and a charcoal disc upon which the incense is placed. This goes in the eastern part of the altar. A glass or goblet is used to symbolise the water element and contains wine or fruit juice. This is used to salute the Gods with a libation (a liquid offering poured out). Place it toward the western section of your altar. Salt signifies the element of earth and this goes in a dish in the northern part of your altar. A small bowl of anointing oil is placed conveniently at the front of the altar. Finally, some reliable matches are required for obvious purposes. If you desire, you can also have statues of the God and Goddess of your choice on the altar, although some witches prefer to omit these or use simple organic items like stones or plants to represent the deities. Go with whatever feels right for you; this is your rite, between the Gods and you.

Around the inner side of the circle place four unlit coloured candles. These go in the four cardinal compass points: red in the south, silver in the west, yellow in the north and blue in the east. Each colour relates to the element which has been found, since time immemorial, to be the most effective one for that purpose.

The Purification Bath

Prior to the rite, prepare a warm bath containing a ritual purification wash (available from authentic occult suppliers). Failing that, use a good handful of sea-salt, pine needles and lemon balm infused for several hours in a bowl of hot water then strained into the bath. Soak yourself in this, visualising all of your problems and worries being absorbed by the water. Then, slowly see a glowing white light surrounding your aura. Imagine it purifying you and preparing you for what is to come. Dry yourself.

RITE OF INITIATION

Walk into the circle from the east, tying the cord (if used) with a figure of eight behind you as you step inside. Light the charcoal disc.

Sit before the altar in silence, meditating on your reasons for being in this particular place at this time. When you feel ready, sprinkle incense on your charcoal disc. Light the altar candle, stare into its blaze and visualise yourself surrounded by this bright light. See it making you pure and feel its warmth penetrating deep within you to the core of your being. Pick up the candle, in its holder, and with both hands hold it high above your head saying:

'Now is the time of my maturity, now is the hour of my wisdom. Great and most powerful Lady, awesome and timeless Lord, come unto me now so that I may know thy holy grace.'

Now take the altar candle to the eastern quarter and light the blue candle from it saying:

'Guardians of the eastern point protect this, my circle.'

Proceed to the southern candle and lighting it say in a clear voice:

'May the fire of illumination blaze forever in my soul - guardian of the south, strengthen my resolve herein.'

Then go over to the silver candle saying:

'Western guardians protect this place and lend thy holy guidance to me here and now.'

Finally, visit the northern candle, light it and say sternly:

'Northern guardian of the winter quarter I call thee to this place and request thy holy protection herein.'

Return to the altar and replace your white candle. Then add a little salt to the water bowl; stir it several times with your index finder in a clockwise (sun-wise) direction saying:

'May this sacred life-fluid command all impurities to flee this holy place.'

As you do this, visualise your energy flowing through your fingers into the water. See the fluid starting to glow brilliant white. Now take the salted water and, walking clock-wise, sprinkle several drops on each quarter of your circle. Return to the altar and anoint yourself by dipping your index finger in the water and rubbing it on you forehead and heart areas. Then, with arms held high, say:

'I stand here naked before thee my Lord and Lady. Long have I travelled the path of life, seeking what I know to be true. I am of the river, I am of the sky, I am of the sun and also of the moon. Without thy holy and most sacred power I am nothing. Thou givest me the will to venture far and the wisdom to realise thy awesome magnitude.'

Pick up the goblet and gently pour a small amount of wine onto the ground (or into a libation dish) saying:

'Great Mother and Father of all things I salute thee.'

Drink some wine from the goblet and visualise it linking you with the rite and your initiation. Next, put your finger into the anointing oil and draw three small pentagrams, one on each nipple and the last on the genitals. This forms a sacred triangle linking to the triple Goddess of life, death and rebirth. As you perform this action say:

'Divine Mother of the Earth, great Father of the sky, I welcome thee into my heart and soul for this is where thou belongest. Accept me as I am, a simple Pagan, into thy guiding light.'

Hold your arms high with and eyes raised, visualise a shaft of golden light descending from above passing into your forehead and travelling throughout your being. Then say, with complete sincerity, in a loud, clear voice:

'In this consecrated place at this sacred time, I dedicate my whole, true being to thee my Lord and Lady. This I do with pure heart, love and sincerity.'

If you are truly genuine in your work, at this time you may feel emotion swell up within you. Do not try and suppress it but instead go with the flow and do whatever feels natural such as cry, laugh, dance or sing. If you feel like being reflective or quiet then that's fine too. Just be as the Gods want you to be because you are about to start a brand new life.

Finally, raise your arms high one more time and say:

'From this moment on, I shall be reborn as a follower of the Old Gods. All-powerful and knowing Lord and Lady, I thank thee both for bringing me to this sacred place in time. I have found my true home within thy holy grace. Be my guiding light from now to eternity. So be it.'

Now thank the quarter-guardians and put out their flames but allow the altar candle to burn itself out. Then say:

'The circle is now opened once again.'

Untie your circle cord and step out into a new existence. You are now a *bona fide* witch, Pagan and a practitioner of the Old Religion. Always remember your initiation, for if performed sincerely it is as legitimate as any created by any coven or group - and in some cases more so. This special spiritual relationship is between you and your Gods, and cannot be broken by anyone but you.

This ritual can be adapted to suit personal interpretation. The terms 'Lord and Lady' may be changed for deity names that appeal to you. They could be Apollo and Venus, Odin and Freya, Lugh and Coventina, Pan and Aphrodite or any other pair that instinctively feels right. As long as you are happy with them then that's all that matters. Paying homage and worshipping deities with alien-feeling names is quite useless, for the connection between you and them will never be strong, so get this essential point sorted out as soon as you possibly can.

Now that you have dedicated yourself to the Old Gods you can feel much more at home with your magical workings. Many folk discover the deep sense of purpose that comes from the authenticity of self-initiation and it is this sincerity that is the key. It is possible to practice magic without such devotion, yet witchcraft and Paganism of any denomination is first and foremost a way of honouring the Gods, with magic coming second.

CONSECRATING YOUR MAGICAL TOOLS

Place your object, such a new bell or athame, on a flat stone or other suitable surface that has previously been cleansed with salted water. Now say:

'I bless thee with the earth.'

Next, sprinkle the object with salted water saying:

'I consecrate thee to water.'

Pass it through incense and say:

'May air bless thy being.'

Then pass it through a candle flame saying:

'In the names of the lord and lady I bless thee with fire.'

When this action is done, kiss the item and keep it upon your person for a day so that it may absorb your vibrations and vice versa. It is now consecrated and linked to you on deeper levels.

All altar equipment should be blessed like this before use to remove stray psychic vibrations. Wrap your objects in black silk cloth after this rite to protect them.

RITE FOR SELF-CLEANSING AND PROTECTION

This is a rite that can be performed at any time or place. It is, however, most effective if done on the waning moon on a Tuesday. It will help you to feel better in many ways and allow you to overcome negative energies. Choose a quiet place where you will not be disturbed.

Face the eastern direction and draw, with your leading index finger or athame, a bright golden pentagram in the clear space before you. Visualise this sign burning bright in front of your face whilst saying:

'In the eastern quarter do I draw on the power of air.'

Now imagine a circle of blue energy bursting out of the pentagram and encapsulating your being. Feel this penetrating your aura.

Next, face the south, draw a blazing pentagram and say:

'Creatures of fire, lend me your assistance.'

This time feel the red triangle of the fire element descend upon you.

Then face the west, draw another five-pointed star and say:

'Divine spirits of water balance the forces within.'

Visualise a silvery crescent of power entering your body going from the top of your head to the tips of your toes.

Then turn clockwise once more and face the north. Draw the sacred star and say:

'Guardians of the earthly winter quarter cleanse my being.'

See the glowing yellow square of energy roar into your essence.

Finally, turn to the east once again. Now cup your hands together as if scooping up water. Take a deep breath and as you slowly exhale, visualise a black ball of negativity coming from your mouth into your hands. When you have this image clearly state the following in a very stern voice:

'Mars, lord of banishment, lord of the destructive realm, take this evil from my body. Take it back from whence it came.'

With this, suddenly cast the ball into the air above your head and see it shooting into the distant sky to be exploded into infinity.

Then you should conclude your rite by saying:

'May this evil be transformed into healing energy. I am now free of all impurities.'

Walk away and feel the benefit of your work, which will continue throughout the day ahead.

SEASONAL RITES

Many Pagans prefer to stick to the usual much-written about Celtic festivals such as Imbolc, Samhain etc, however what we shall study next will be a Classical Roman variation on this popular theme.

First let us perform a late summer seasonal rite in honour of the great god Jupiter. August is the time of the *Vinalia* of Jupiter, so this is a grand time to perform this particular rite.

Drape a white or gold cloth over your altar. Strew it with wild berries, fruit and flowers or any other natural items that catch the essence of the season. The altar holds two candles, one blue to symbolise Jupiter's realm of the sky, and one red for the summer. Use incense that links to the god or the seasonal cycle. Have a small bell on the altar and pour red wine into your goblet. Finally, an athame is required which should have been consecrated prior to usage. After the purification bath, enter the circle and perform the salute as previously given for the protective guardian(s) of each specific quarter. Approach the altar of Jupiter and say:

'All hail to the lord of the sky. Thou art the master who grants rain to the crops so that thy children may feast.'

With this, ring the bell thrice, hold up the goblet and say:

'Now is the time of the harvest. Now is the time of the ripening vine. Jupiter Optimus Maximus, greatest and best, bestow thy sacred force unto this wine.'

With this statement, visualise Jupiter's power streaming into the wine as a beam of electric blue light. Drink solemnly from the cup while feeling this blue energy flood every part of your being. Replace the goblet and put some incense in your burner as an offering to the God, then raise your athame and continue:

'I give thanks for thy blessings which are symbolised in the rich harvest around. The joy and peace of thy bounty pale all other things into insignificance. In the rich thunder rains I feel thy glory. In the hot summer wind I feel thy power. My lord Jupiter, may the holy force in thee and thy consort the divine Juno be forever within me.'

Now light the blue and red candles on the altar and say:

'Here is a token of the summer, here is a token of my Lord '

Raise the two candles very slowly and continue:

'As these holy flames glow bright may in like fashion my love and power follow. All hail to thee most awesome lord Jupiter, grand master this day of the new made wine.'

Finally, replace the two candles and ring the bell three times. Finish by saluting the guardians of the quarters and open the circle. You now have a simple method of Pagan worship, which can be adapted to suit all other deities. Remember that sincerity is the most important aspect in all of your working. With the above rites we have briefly explored the possibilities of magical practice.

Chapter 4
MAGIC

Working magic and casting spells are deeply beneficial experiences. The spell connects us with the Gods. With patience and correct timing I find that most workings come to fruition. However, even if I get things wrong there is always a sense of increased awareness and heightened spirituality following a rite, so positive magical growth come from rituals that may not seem to hit their desired mark. Sincerity of will is the key to success and growth in magic.

We don't create magical energy: it's already there to start with like electricity. We heighten or raise it with increased emotion then, with correct timing, re-direct it to its goal. Sometimes we miss our goal but with skill and foresight often as not score a bull's eye and achieve the desired effect.

The old occult maxim is worth heeding here - *'To Know, To Dare, To Will and to Keep Silent'*. To know is to have the relevant knowledge to perform the magical task at hand. To dare is to have the courage to take our destiny into our own hands, enter into the cosmic whirlpool and act accordingly. To will is to realise that we must hone our will power into a formidable weapon for future growth. Silence is, as they say, golden. The magical braggart quickly dilutes any previously effective works and his/ her efforts soon lose momentum. This does not only apply to magic, we all know that little men tend to shout the loudest and are frequently the ones that most ignored by the crowd the most. On higher levels of existence the Gods also tend to turn their backs on the rowdy boaster; all planes of reality are interconnected - as above, so it is below.

To know magic is to open your true self up to the beautiful and awesome power of the Gods. This cannot be fully appreciated on the logical, conscious level; when we leave the mundane-thinking behind and give ourselves up to the Gods then, and only then, do we honestly begin to understand the real nature of raw magical power: a power of which we are a small but vitally important part.

Magic is free, it is majestic and it is the birthright of every single person on this planet. To refuse to use it, or worse still ignore it, is to deny your own spiritual advancement and source of self-liberation.

It is not the purpose of this book to delve deeply into magical work; however the following will serve as a brief primer for the eager newcomer.

THE TIMING OF MAGIC

The timing of magic is especially important. For creative magic we must work with the waxing moon but for banishing magic we work on the waning moon. The ancients found that certain days of the week were best for certain workings:

- MONDAY: The best time for spells of divination, visions and fascination. This day, as the name (moon-day) suggests, belongs to the lunar goddess.
- TUESDAY: The period to banish all ills and negativity. Tuesday is the time of the war god Mars.
- WEDNESDAY: Belongs to the god of merchants, Mercury. A good day for working career and business spells.
- THURSDAY: A day for wealth and prosperity; the day of Jupiter, great lord of the Roman pantheon.
- FRIDAY: The best time for romance. This is the day of Venus, goddess of love and beauty.
- SATURDAY: Saturn's day is the best time to perform spells connected to greater wisdom and new projects. Saturn is the deity linked to sowing, so it is an excellent time to put fresh ideas into practice.
- SUNDAY: This day belongs to gods linked to the sun. A great time to work for financial success and all aspects connected to growth and prosperity.

Hours of the day are also very important to successful magical work and it is advisable for any student to purchase tables of these periods from a reputable occult supplier. For the sake of simplicity, I shall give you an example for a period connected with each day. This will enable you to work your spell at the correct time. The third hour after sundown on each day is the period linked to the deity connected with that particular day. This is useful to remember if you wish to work at night. If you prefer to operate in the day then use the first hour after sunrise to link with the God or Goddess of that actual day.

If this seems overtly complicated then consider the following. It is perhaps Friday and you want to work love magic. Get up early and catch the first hour as the sun breaks over the horizon to do your spell. This is the hour of Venus. Alternatively, you may wish to do a banishing rite on the correct day, which is Tuesday. You want to do it at night so you must wait for the third hour after the sun has set. It is quite simple once you get the hang of it and well worth the extra trouble involved. Magic can work without this added labour yet why not give yourself every opportunity of success?

The Athame

Witches usually possess a special working ceremonial tool known as an *'Athame.'* This is a knife which is used for various ritual purposes such as to carve names on candles etc. If possible you should strive to fashion your own athame or at least buy one from an occult supplier then perhaps etch your own symbols into the handle to make it unique to you. Excellent details regarding making your own athame can be found in *Buckland's Complete Book of Witchcraft* by Raymond Buckland. Llewellyn, St Paul, 1992

Spell Working

There are many ways to perform a spell but here we shall just use a simple candle-working as an example. We are going to do a spell for assistance in writing skills, so we need to call upon the lord, Mercury.

Cover the altar with a yellow cloth (yellow is the colour associated with Mercury). At the far corners of the altar place two unlit yellow candles in safe holders. Carve your name on an additional white candle and put this to the front right-hand side. To the left place a brown candle. This represents concentration and is an excellent colour to assist you in absorbing skill and knowledge. Use Mercury incense and have candle-anointing oil to hand in a small vessel.

Following a purification bath, enter the circle and summon the four guardians of the quarters and light them a candle (see the chapter on ritual for further information) then meditate upon the purpose of the rite before you.

First, 'magnetise' all the altar candles with the oil. This is done by gripping the base of the candle with your left hand whilst stroking oil from the centre with the right hand index finger, up to the top. Then change hands and grip the candle at the top with the right hand whilst rubbing with the left index linger from the centre to its base. This action carries your auric powers, via the oil, directly to the candle.

Whilst you do this say for each candle something like:

'From me into thee, success is now assured.'

Now light all candles except the brown object and white subject candle. When this is done, with arms held high, say in a loud, clear voice:

'Mercury, from the corners of the universe I summon thee. Mercury, from the corners of the universe I summon thee. Lord Mercury be with me now in this place.'

Now visualise, with all your power, Mercury coming before you in classical form. See him getting closer and closer as you call to him. Feel his energy around you say:

'Lord of great wisdom. Lord of great skill. Awesome lord of knowledge, I feel thy power taking over mine centre and being. Join me now; join me now; join me now.'

Do this with great feeling and honesty and do not worry if you begin to feel somewhat light-headed or over-excited. This is just the God's energy altering your consciousness, which is desirable if you are to achieve success. Go along with the energy of the god-form and let it all happen. If you feel like jumping, chanting or singing then by all means do so, for this will help you to raise more power. Let the God take you over and go with the flow. When you feel full of the God's power say:

'Magnificent lord of the hidden knowledge, great cup-bearer to the high gods, grant thy awesome power to my spell.'

With this request, light the brown (object) candle with the white (subject) candle that symbolises yourself. Then firmly say:

'From this moment on, thy holy power shall work through me from this place. The grace of thy holy intelligence shall guide mine hand whenever I have need.'

Allow the wax of the two candles to intermingle and visualise the perfect image of the outcome you desire for your spell. When you are satisfied with this vision, give the God your thanks with a small libation of wine (libation is the pouring of a liquid offering to the gods). Then drink from the goblet, raise your hands and say:

'Mercury, I thank thee with all mine heart in the sure knowledge that with thy sacred force this work will come to fruition.'

Finally, end the working by stating:

'Mercury, return now to thy foundations.
Mercury, return now to thy foundations.
Mercury, return now to thy foundations.'

Now, allow yourself a little time to return to your normal mundane consciousness. Do not be in a great rush. Permit the object and subject candles to burn out in their own good time and salute the four guardians of the watchtowers. Extinguish the yellow altar candles and open the circle.

The magic is now set in motion. Never allow any negative thoughts to stray into your mind about your working. Go your way quietly in the sure knowledge that your spell will materialise.

Never try to be greedy with your magic, only ask for what is truly needed, for the universe will refuse to bend in ways that are unsuited to your own abilities and skills. Genuine need and emotion are vital to successful spells and those performed without these two vital factors will never result in total success. One step at a time is the best philosophy.

As they rightly say, *'Rome wasn't built in a day.'* Have faith in your work and allow the Gods to show you the way in all things. Your magic will work if you permit it to, although it can frequently be in ways that are not expected. This is the beauty and mystery of spells. In similar a fashion to the angler who casts his bait into unknown waters, we never quite know just what we will catch with our workings. One thing is quite certain; the Gods do have a strong sense of humour at times, which you will do well to remember. Always believe in their capability to assist you if a genuine need is present. Never, ever mess them around as they do not suffer fools gladly. If magic is too difficult, tiring and complicated for you at this time in your life then *leave it alone*.

The Old Gods deserve our respect, and only an idiot will take up a magical life for fun. To perform magic in a frivolous manner is asking for trouble and can lead to unbalance. This is one of the main reasons why magic often gets dire reports with the sensation-seeking press. The ignorant fool who fancies a little dabble and ends up depressed, afraid or more stupid than he was before, wishing to gain sympathy or even notoriety for his own inadequacies, then blames the Gods and the magic for his own failure and low condition. Respect the awesome power of the Gods and celebrate their grandeur. Do this and they will repay you in manifold ways you cannot yet fully comprehend.

Chapter 5
SEASONAL FESTIVALS

Midsummer

Of all the archetypal symbols none remains more deeply ingrained in our subconscious than the circle or the wheel., emblematic of the continuity of existence. It is a sign of the lunar and solar principles and it is a symbol of infinity because it has no beginning and no end.

As a representation of the sun, the symbol of the wheel is at its most potent during the Midsummer Solstice, a time when the sun is at its highest point in the heavens. Now all natural growth is at the zenith of its potential. The wheel of the year, from this day on, can only roll downhill towards autumn and the bleak death of winter. Whether we like it or not, we are all an essential part of the organic universal plan.

The Roman goddess of fate and luck was known as Fortuna, hence the other name for chance, fortune. She is often depicted with a ship's rudder, sphere, cornucopia or wheel. Fortuna humbles even the highest members of a society; great emperors would often display images of her in their private chambers to remind them of her power, for without luck they would have nothing. The Romans built eight separate temples to honour her in their city. Fortuna's Temple at Antium in Latium was so popular that large quantities of gifts and offerings were sent in from all over the country by worshippers hoping to attract her favour. Fortuna had a feast day shortly after the Midsummer Solstice in June, when slaves would also be welcomed into the celebrations; she could even smile kindly on the most downtrodden. The Wheel of Fortuna is represented in the tenth card of the tarot's Major Arcana. Even now, who does not rejoice over good luck or protest over misfortune? Gamblers still watch, with bated breath, as the roulette wheel spins for or against them.

Numerius Sufficius, a native of Latium, was troubled by a recurring dream. It led him to a rock where he discovered wooden lots, small pieces of oak which had ancient characters inscribed on them. These were used to receive divinely inspired predictions from the goddess. The final act of trusting one's destiny to the goddess by drawing lots is a custom that has survived through thousands of years to the present day.

The association of the wheel and circle and Midsummer Pagan fire-festivals is very ancient indeed. Long before Christianity, the Neolithic peoples worshipped their gods and buried their dead at stone circles. The day of the longest-sun was a sacred time, a time to propitiate the Old Gods to ensure a successful harvest and future growth. Midsummer Eve fires would be lit high on hills to encourage the sun. Our ancient forefathers needed rain as well as sun to achieve satisfactory crops and many old customs point to this fact. One old tradition involved a large straw bound wheel being ignited and then rolled down a hillside into a river. This event was symbolic of the sun's energy intermingling with the element of water to produce good growth in vegetation.

The Church naturally saw this old Pagan festival as an excellent event to convert into one of its own, hence the water associations with a baptising saint. The early Church decided to hold the feast-day of Saint John the Baptist at Midsummer.

Lughnasadh

Our ancient Celtic ancestors celebrated the initiation of August with the feast of the god Lugh. Lughnasadh (meaning 'Commemoration of Lugh') was one of the four great Celtic annual festivals, the others being Imbolg (February 2nd) Beltaine (30th April) and Samhain (31st October).

In Gaelic mythology, Lugh is portrayed as battle-leader of the Tuatha de Danann. He had many talents: his athletic prowess and commanding skills earned him the titles *Samildanach* ('God of All Arts') and *Lugh-Lamhfhada* ('Lugh the Long-Handed' or 'Far-Shooter'), referring to his expertise with the rod sling with which defeated the Fomorian giant, Balor. Balor was Lugh's grandfather, a dreadful cyclopean figure who needed four men to lift his baleful eye which could kill with a single glance. Lugh defeated him by piercing his evil-eye with a stone from his magical sling-shot. This tale points to Lugh's popular light-defeating-dark aspect, a common theme in all ancient mythology.

Lugh was revered by all the Celtic peoples. The Welsh knew him as Llew Llaw Gyffes. The Celts of the continent called him Lugus, leaving his name in the cities of Lugudunum (now Lyons), the town of Lugus [Laon] and Leyden among others. At various times, Lugh has been depicted as a deity of fire, corn, marriage and the sun. This has lead to some confusion as to his true identity and mythological status.

The worship of Lugh first arrived in this land with the Goidelic (Gaelic) Celts around 600 BCE. This invasion was followed two hundred years later by the Brythonic (Cornish and Welsh) Celts. Lugh was very much a hero-god of the Hercules type: Llew or Lleu means 'Lion' and 'Light' respectively. Great tales of his adventures would be told on cold nights around the comforting warmth of the hearth fire, giving hope to the tribe in the hard periods of winter's chill.

This god was particularly venerated at harvest time, his powerful energy seen within in the golden fields of summer. In the dying corn of August, Lugh becomes the god of death and resurrection. Lugh's sphere altered somewhat with the arrival of the Roman legions under Caesar. The Latin conquerors eventually amalgamated their own deities with those of the Celtic peoples and Lugh was no exception; he was cleverly blended with the Roman and Greek Apollo, a solar deity. His feast day was later rededicated to the deified emperor Augustus and the rich month of harvest became known as August.

The question arises to whether or not Lugh was actually a sun god proper. I believe that originally he was not, but with the later development of agriculture (dependant upon the sun) he evolved into a deity of increasing solar force. History testifies to the fact that all deities go through cycles of transformation with cultural developments. The personification of Lugh as a deity of the ripening cornfields in August gives us clear evidence of our ancestors' deep desire to link with nature.

Lughnasadh was Christianised under the name Lammas Day, from the old Anglo-Saxon word *Hlaf-mass* ('Loaf-Mass') which relates to the older *Lughomass* (Lugh's-Mass). Lugh, like other Celtic deities, was taken by later Christian Norman romancers and given a new role in mythology. Lugh's heroic deeds were skilfully euphemised into the legendary figure of Sir Lancelot. [8]

Yuletide and the Saturnalia

The contemporary Christian feast day of Christmas originates in the vast storehouse of ancient Pagan mythology. The actual date of Jesus Christ's birthday is unknown. Even the gospels fail to specify the exact time of his birth. In fact, the Church only set up the official date in 273 CE. The early Church, ever enthusiastic to win converts from the old Earth-orientated faiths, decided to adopt the native midwinter festival and claim it as its own.

Thousands of years before the Christian cult arose our Pagan forefathers were celebrating the happy feast of the Midwinter Solstice. Everywhere people honoured the birth of the sun god under his numerous titles and names.

Midwinter marked the period when the sun was at its lowest point in the sky. This truth was acknowledged as the time of new birth; from now onward the days would grow lighter as the power of the great life-giver increased. Christianity merely took the name 'sun' and transformed it into 'son' (as in Son of God) so as to give the new faith from the East a more acceptable face for our Pagan ancestors.

Most Christmas traditions and customs are based on the old Roman feast of the Saturnalia, which was enjoyed for seven days toward the end of December. During the celebration of the god Saturn all schools, courts and businesses would remain closed. Slaves and masters would reverse roles, with masters serving their subordinates at table. During the Saturnalia, slaves were allowed to wear the small cap known as a *pileus*, the Roman sign of a freeman. This is a detail worth remembering when people next enter into the party spirit and don silly hats at their Xmas Feast. Army officers still serve their minions at Xmas dinner and the charity aspect of the Solstice is common even today; employers worldwide still give large parties for their workers and folk exchange loving presents.

The word *Yule* comes from the old Viking *Iul* meaning 'wheel', Yule being the lowest point in the sun's travel through the wheel of the year. A Yule log was traditionally cut from the oak-tree, a wood sacred to the thunder god Thor or Thunor. The Yule log, after being charred by fire, was believed to protect a dwelling from lightening strike.

Mistletoe was seen as an all-healing plant and was sacred to the Norse deity Balder. It was used by Druidic priests to promote fertility and so it is still used in a magical sense i.e. kissing under the mistletoe.

Holly is a customary part of Yuletide and has traditional connections: it is sacred to Saturn, god of the dying year, and Romans hung it outside their houses to avert psychic attack, lightening and evils of any kind. Today's Father Christmas image is based upon the Holly-King figure of Odin, the Norse father god who rode through the night's sky, not on a reindeer but a rapid white charger.

Xmas trees originate from the ancient rites of the Phrygian mother goddess Cybele, whose worship was taken to Rome in 204 BCE. A pine tree was felled and placed within her temple, then adorned with beautiful flowers and coloured wools. It is quite likely that the tree custom travelled with the legions into Germanic localities and amalgamated with native tradition there at some later date. We should possibly give credit for the tree's modern-day usage in celebration to Drusus the Elder, who undertook a military campaign for Roman domination against the Germanic and Raetian tribes in 15 BCE.

Any seriously impartial examination of the historical side of Christmas clearly reveals that Christianity has no right whatsoever to claim sole monopoly of the resurrection god. The Christian re-born sun-god myth is but the latest in a long line of deity modifications. Attis, Adonis, Sol, Mithras and numerous other Gods were celebrated during seasonal solar cycles long before the Jesus story was created.

Yuletide and the Midwinter Solstice is an indispensable element of our Pagan year. It connects us with the wondrous seasonal energies of the planet of which we are all an integral part. We should always celebrate and enjoy it to the full.

Today's thinking classical and Roman Pagan should have no trouble whatsoever in developing an individual winter celebration to honour the Old Gods. There is a wealth of mythological data to draw upon making this task all the easier.

January, New Year and the Compitalia
After the festivities of Yuletide and the Midwinter Solstice, we quickly arrive at the start of the contemporary year. I emphasise the word 'contemporary' because calendars have so frequently changed over the centuries. The pastoral, pre-

Christian Celts regarded Halloween as the end of summer and the beginning of winter. It marked the start of the New Year. When we forget the man-made calendar and take a long hard look at nature's moods, this old method of time calculation begins to make a great deal of sense. At the beginning of the modern New Year celebrations, trees have already started to produce swelling buds and migratory fish like salmon and sea trout have long since dropped their eggs in highland streams. Nature celebrates her own New Year as the Celts did, several months before today's more thoughtless event. Many parts of our modern culture are thinly based on the vast wisdom of our ancient Pagan ancestors.

January gets its name from the Roman god of doorways and new ventures, Janus, who was usually portrayed with two heads, one looking to the past whilst the other viewed the future. Some ancient scholars have preferred to think of Janus as watching over the commencement and finish of the sun's travel though the daily sky. Janus then, lends his name to the year's beginning and, like us, he looks nostalgically back at the past and into the exciting future to come.

The Romans held a feast day on the 12th of January (and also on the 6th of March) called the *Compitalia*. This festival was performed in honour of the household gods, the Lares. These much-loved deities were two in number and their father was Mercury, messenger of the gods. On this occasion, masters would serve meals to their servants, as they did in December at the Saturnalia. Special incense was burnt on the Lares' altar and oil lamps would light the chilled night air. Tree branches decorated the rooms and hallways, while small images of the Lares adorned tables. The Lares were also venerated in May when bright flowers featured in the celebrations. The name Compitalia relates to the title *Lares-Compitales*, protective deities of the crossroads. Thus an important part of the Compitalia itself was celebrated at places where pathways crossed. The name Lares comes from the Etruscan word *lars* which means 'conductor' or 'leader'. Images of straw men and the dried heads of poppy flowers were a favourite offering to these Gods.

The wise old Romans were exceptionally dutiful, having a deity for everything and its action. Most accidents seem to happen in the home. Maybe a kind word with the Lares this New Year is just the thing needed to avert misfortune. Now where did I put those poppy heads?

February, the Feralia and the Terminalia

February is often a cold, bleak month when little seems to stir in the natural world. It gains its name from the Etruscan god of the underworld and purification, Februus. He is often equated with the Greek gods Pluto and Hades and the Gallic god of riches, Dis, cognate with the Roman Orcus. On the 17th or 21st of February, Februus was venerated at a feast known as the Feralia. During this event, marriages were not allowed, all the shrines and temples of other Gods were closed and gifts were taken to the graves of relatives and friends.

The *Manes* (souls of the departed) were believed to hover around the monuments and graves of the dead, thus the presents served as a token of respect and propitiation for these spirits. The Manes held much power in the underworld, and only a fool would fail to give them the reverence they deserved. Contemporary man can learn a lot about his subconscious fears of death and dying by relating to this ancient festival. The number three was considered sacred to the Manes, and because of this they were always invoked three times. Gravestones were frequently inscribed with the prefix DM standing for *Di Manes* or *Di-Manibus* which is Latin for 'The Good Gods'.

The celebration of the *Feralia* was also called the *Februa*. The great, powerful goddess Juno was frequently invoked under this title. Her influence, like that Dis, also extended over riches. The purification aspect of this festival remains with us today; we still feel the urge, with the dawning of the lighter nights, to get stuck in and have an energetic bout of spring-cleaning. The difference is that the Romans also did their spring cleaning on the spiritual level.

Moving to the 23rd of this month, we discover a feast called the *Terminalia*, which as its name suggests, was sacred to Terminus, god of limits and boundaries. Numa, the legendary second king of Rome, introduced the feast of the Terminalia. Terminus was originally depicted by a simple marker-stone. Later on he was portrayed as a human head without arms and legs to show that, like limit marks, he never moved his position. It is interesting to note here that Jupiter, the all-powerful king of the Gods, was often called Terminalus and he presided over boundaries long before Terminus did. It is quite probable then that this aspect of Jupiter later evolved into a separate deity. Offerings of wine, oil, flowers and milk were given to Terminus at the Terminalia. So hallowed was the head of Terminus, that should another man foolishly attempt to steal or even move it, he faced public execution. This proves how important property was to the pragmatic Roman mind. Terminus had no time for infringements of his law; his wrath was swift and very effective indeed.

Many of today's Pagans view early pre-Spring Equinox feasts such as the Terminalia as a time to synchronise with the growing cosmic energies. It is a time to plan carefully for the future with increasing optimism. The spiritual level of existence is just as important as the material and vice versa, so to neglect one aspect jeopardises the other.

The first gentle increase of light, the rich colour of the crocus flowers and the sticky, bursting buds of the horse-chestnut tree give hope for the warm, lengthening days to come. Soon the glorious sun will bring forth life and new growth. Every plant, tree and animal will be ready to greet this time-honoured event. Contemporary man must shake off his self-inflicted, materialistic slumber and synchronise himself to the seasonal forces of nature, just as his ancient forefathers did. Failure to do so will result in a loss of essential at-one-ment with Mother Earth. We too must wake up to the annual universal energies.

March

March is named after the Roman god of vegetation and war, Mars. This month was vital to the ancients as it was deemed to be the first month of the new season; January and February were initially believed to be rather static months with little significance being allotted to them.

On the 14th day of the month a celebration called the *Equiria* was held. This festival was sacred to Mars and great horse races were run in the Campus Martius. The March Equiria was in fact the second festival of this name, the first having been held on February 27th. The legendary Romulus (brother of Remus and son of Mars) instituted these two events. During the Equiria all manner of articles relating to the cavalry units were lustrated and purified.

The horse was one of the animals held sacred to Mars, the others being the wolf, vulture, magpie and dog. The horse is associated with Mars not only because of its connection with combat, but also because of its earlier origins as a beast of burden in agricultural use. How many punters, preparing for make or break on the Grand National, ever pondered on the ancient spiritual link to their sport?

On the 19th day of the month the 'sacred shield' (*Ancile* or *Ancyle*) received great attention and devotion. The Ancile fell from the heavens during the reign of King Numa. He informed the Romans that the very safety and fate of their empire depended upon it. Numa had eleven copies of the shield made to thwart any attempts to steal it. Special warrior priests called *Salii* were installed in the temple of Vesta to guard the Ancile. These priests of Mars came from noble families and their feasts were lavish affairs. They adorned themselves in bright red tunics fastened with purple belts and carried rods and shields. The Salii were twelve in number (one for each shield). This would suggest that twelve is a sacred number of protection, passed down from one ancient culture to the next. Scarlet and red are the colours of warrior gods, and as such belong to the realm of death and destruction. Red is also the colour of life-blood which gives us vitality and new energy. It is the colour of the rose of Venus and the purity marked by the rising sun. With life there is also death and vice versa; we cannot have one without the other.

Modern Pagans, because of their close links with the Earth, continue to synchronise with the same natural green energies emerging in March, the promising month of new growth. This is an especially invigorating period that links us to

Mars, the god of creative and destructive life-force who gives his name to the month. A ritual for this period should accentuate optimism, for now is the time to sow the seeds (on all levels of existence) for summer's bounty to come.

April: the Parilia, Vinalia and Veneralia

The month of April gains its name from the Roman word *aprilis* which comes from the word *aperire* meaning 'to open' because April is the time when birds hatch their chicks, animals mate, buds swell into young leaves and new life begins.

The first day of the month is known to us as April Fool's Day. In France, a gullible person caught by a prankster's trick was called *un poisson d' Avril* ('an April fish'). The ancients held this day, the *Veneralia*, sacred to Venus, goddess of love. During her feast, worshippers would wash the statue of the goddess and hang beautiful flowers about it. Tricks were also played on the unwary as part of the celebration. Venus was originally a patron of seeds, flowers and spring; her later association with love came around 217 BCE when she was equated with the Greek Aphrodite.

Water is necessary to make seeds become flowers, and the fish was a sacred symbol of Venus. The northern equivalent of Venus is Frejya or Freya, who gives her name to Friday. The Christian practice of eating fish on a Friday is also adopted from much older traditions sacred to Venus; this was the day for abstaining from devouring the sacred food of Venus. The early Christian Church subverted the tradition, they *eat* fish on Fridays. Modern Pagans smile when they see a Christian-owned vehicle displaying the old fish sign!

On Saint George's Day, we see another adoption of Pagan tradition. It occurs at the same period as the *Parilia*, 21st April. The Parilia or *Palilia* was sacred to Pales, goddess of shepherds and herders. During the feast, farmers would drive their flocks and herds between blazing fires and fumigate them with rosemary, laurel and sulphur to purify them and ensure strong offspring. Humans would also leap over small fires of straw and dance around them throughout the night, making merry. Offerings to Pales consisted of milk and millet wafers, which were given in the hope of keeping dangerous wolves away from the flocks and to avert disease.

The Palilia is also the anniversary of the building of Rome by Romulus. Romulus investigated Tuscan customs in order to discover the best sort of ceremonies to use for his new city. Accordingly, he gained vital ritual knowledge from the older peoples of that place which they had, in turn, received from Janus, the god of new beginnings. The first wine of the new season was always offered to Janus.

Venus shared a feast - though on two separate days - with Jupiter, called the *Vinalia*. Her day occurred on the same date originally as the later St. George's Day, while Jupiter's took place in August. Wine was freely distributed to the local people from their temples. Prior to this rite, a wine libation was poured on the earth in honour of Venus.¹ The goddess Venus was also offered expensive gifts of roses, myrtle and sweet scented incense at the Vinalia.

Venus travelled in an ivory chariot drawn by swans. Swans are often associated with love deities such as Angus, the Celtic god of love who once turned into a swan. The gentle dove is another sacred symbol of the goddess that was adopted by the early Church and made into its own.

The beautiful April festivals of the love goddess give us a rare insight into the depth of the spiritual wisdom of our Pagan forefathers. Celebrate the growing energies in April and let your spirit free. Now is the time for new plans and growth in all aspects of life.

May: the Floralia and Beltane

This lovely month gains its name from the Roman and Greek fertility goddess Maia, mother of the god Mercury. She was equated with Fauna, Cybele and Ops, goddesses who were greatly cherished and respected by the masses.

Fauna's feast day was held on the first night of May. It was a sacred occasion exclusive to women, while the men honoured Fauna's male consort Faunus. During Fauna's celebration wine and music blended with magical ritual in a joyous medley of sound and veneration.

From the 28th April to the 3rd of May, a festival called the *Floralia* was celebrated in honour of the Sabine Flora, goddess of flowering gardens. Virgil wrote that young folk would venture out at Floralia to pick summer flowers from field, wood and meadow. Singing and dancing took place and this natural Pagan love of life has come down to us today in the form of contemporary May Day celebrations. May Queen and King parades can easily be traced back to ancient Rome and beyond.

Roman children adorned little clay statues of the goddess with wild blossoms as a token of love and respect. (The early Church cleverly swapped her image for one of the Virgin Mary). Flora was frequently depicted as a young maiden wearing a floral crown. She had two major temples at Rome, so it is clear that her devotion from the people was regarded as a threat by the Church fathers. Flora's worship is however not to be crushed so easily as her beauty will forever remain in the hearts of lovers as long as there are still wild May flowers on the uncultivated field and hillside.

The Celtic Mayday is known as *Beltane* and *Beltaine* ('Fire of Bel'). Bel or Bile is associated with the Roman Pluto and Dis-Pater, lord of the underworld and death; numerous legends claim he arrived from Spain (which is actually a euphemism for the Celtic Hades).

On May-Eve, all household fires would be extinguished then later rekindled from a great hilltop blaze (the Druids believed that it was sacrilegious to worship the Gods in dwellings made by mortal man). Beltane was the start of the Celtic summer and the blaze connected with the increasing solar power needed to sustain life. A brand was brought to each homestead as a vital magical token of new life. The mysterious green life-energy was flowing in nature and it couldn't be ignored.

Today, the very same power of summer's increasing light that our ancestors celebrated is with us again each Beltane. Man-made religions have come and gone in their multitudes, yet spring still slowly turns into summer just as it always has. Our forbears didn't need to have faith in anything but the natural divinity residing within nature's many moods, which they connected with every day of their lives. Each Mayday, we too must remember the Pagan wisdom of the old ones and re-connect with the healing power of nature.

The above listing of Pagan festivals will hopefully encourage the student to examine this topic further. If we look deeply enough, all ancient celebrations relate to nature and our own place within the cosmic whole. It is vital to remember that Pagan worship is not in any way doctrinal. It is a sparkling gem of self-liberation that refuses to be placed in the box of staid orthodoxy. This is why it has withstood the severest assaults of monotheistic oppression throughout the ages and always will. Authentic Paganism, performed with a sincere heart, will never be the spiritual opiate of the masses. Real Paganism is very much the path of the liberated 'lone wolf.'

The gods of the Old Religion are evident in each shaft of forest sunlight, each bolt of white nocturnal lightening, each wave that crashes upon an ancient shoreline, and each opening bloom on a frosty spring morning.

EPILOGUE

It is the author's sincerest wish that this book will enlighten the seeker and hopefully guide him or her into the exciting ways of individual Pagan practice and exploration.

At the end of the day, labels such as Pagan, mystic, witch, shaman and so on are altogether quite meaningless. What really matters is personal commitment to your quest for wisdom and self-realisation on all levels. Unfortunately, labels are often used to impress the naïve and gain brownie points in polite company. Labels are used to command power and respect from others – this may ultimately lead to corruption. Personal insecurity and gross inadequacies are frequently masked behind grand sounding titles like high priest and priestess. We see the same situation in all belief systems and the sight of a disgraced bishop or deacon in orthodox Christian circles is sadly all too common. The genuine wise-person will have none of this point scoring. A serious witch and Pagan who is close to nature needs no authorisation or blessing from other humans to connect honestly with his and her own God and Goddess.

Regrettably, many people who are attracted to mystery faiths bring their previous monotheistic indoctrinations with them which eventually taints the authentic nature-based roots of Paganism. This is music to the ears of the forces of missionary evangelism. Uncertainty leads to division, which in turn causes the bewildered seeker to return to the (wrongly) perceived safety of his or her own monotheistic upbringing. Occasionally (and more insidiously) the monotheistic-minded pretender who has dipped his toes into the waters of Paganism and found them rather too hot for his taste will 'cry wolf'. We see this still occurs regularly with money-spinning sensationalist tabloid stories like *'Witch Ate My Babies'* or *'My Escape from Black Witches'* and even *'God Saved me from Satan-Sacrifice.'* The list is endless and no evidence is ever forthcoming to substantiate these ludicrous claims which can lead to wholesale intimidation against innocent occult minorities everywhere.

It is important to note that the author makes these observations not out of mere personal opinion but from many years of working at the leading edge of the *Pagan Anti-Defamation Network* frontline. Fortunately, many Pagans are now gaining the measure of the current situation. They are realising that genuine Paganism will never be a faith with a majority following. This is not in any way meant to promote elitism. Magical evolution is a personal quest and every person is at a different stage along the path to divine wisdom. Furthermore, anything existing on a personal basic can never belong to the majority, *en bloc*. Your spiritual perception and awareness belong to you and you alone.

This final thought fittingly brings us right back to the solitary figure with arms outstretched before the sacred Altar of Jupiter: the 'Merlin of the Wild Wood' who feels the night breeze against his chilled face and knows cosmic wisdom from within, the lone witch entranced by the sparkling ripples of a babbling mountain stream.

Always remember that if we don't think for ourselves others will do it for us. This is a fact of life that sets the only true course possible for those rare spirits who passionately desire knowledge. Authentic Paganism is a way of being; it is a great gift that we are all born with. Do not let others waste it for you. It's in the moods of the sky, the flicker of a glowing candle-flame and the cold midnight cries of a fox. Our prime Holy Quest must be to rediscover this ancient sense, this childlike knowing that bypasses the critical, materialist mind.

The Old Gods reside deep within us. They dwell also in the vast uncharted corners of the universe and beyond. Their terrible - yet beautiful - force creates, destroys then creates again all things in existence. They wait, sometimes patiently, sometimes anxiously, for us to give them conscious acknowledgement. In turn they give us great realisation of self and the world we live in. The wondrous Lord and Lady of Paganism are as real today as they have ever been for those exceptional and enlightened people who grant them passage into their hearts, minds and souls.

This particular Pagan journey has run its course.

Now go and start your own.

Appendix 1
A-Z of Roman and other Festivals

AMBARVALIA: In honour of Ceres, two festivals in April and July.

AMBURBIA: Procession around city walls.

ANNA PERRENA: (Festival of) March 15th.

ANTHESPHORIA: In honour of Proserpine (in Sicily).

ANTHESTERIA: Festival of Bacchus (February)

ANTINOEJA: Annual games in honour of Antinous.

ASCOLIA: For Bacchus in December.

AUGUSTA'LIA: Commemorating the return of Augustus.

BACCHANALIA: Four festivals in honour of Bacchus (see Dionysia).

BONA DEA: May 1st.

BRUMALIA: In honour of Bacchus in December.

CAPROTINA: In July for Juno.

CARNA and CARDINEA: In June (the goddess of hinges, entrails and secret body parts).

CEREALIA: April 12th-19th extending over eight days, in honour of Ceres.

CIRCENSES LUDI: 5 days from 15th Sept for Consus (Consualia).

COMPITA'LIA: 12th Jan to 6th March, in honour of the Lares.

DELIA: (Apollo) every fifth year at Delos and at Athens yearly.

DIONYSIA: (see Bacchanalia). 9th-15th March.

ELEUSINIA: 15th-23rd Sept - in honour of Ceres and Proserpine.

FABARIA: 1st JUNE, in honour of Carna (the goddess of hinges).

FAUNALIA SACRA: 5th December, in honour of Faunus.

FERALIA: 17th or 21st February, for eleven days (in honour of Manes).

FLORALIA: 28th April for several days in honour of Flora.

FONTINALIA: 13th OCTOBER, in honour of fountain nymphs.

FORNACALIA: In honour of Fornax (the goddess of baking bread).

FORDICIDIA: 17th Calends of March.

FUGALIA: In honour of the goddess of liberty (See REGIFUGIUM).

FURINALIA: FURINA is the goddess of robbers (in July).

GAMELIA: Three festivals, births weddings and death anniversaries (also on 1st January) - Sacred to Juno.

HALIA and HA'LIA: In honour of the Sun at Rhodes.

HECALESIA: In honour of Jupiter (of Hecale)

HELENIA: In Laconia in honour of Helen.

HECATESIA: In honour of Hecate.

HELLOTIA: Two festivals in honour of Minerva and Europa.

HEPH'STIA: In honour of Vulcan at Athens, a race with torches - (See PROTERVIA, VULCANIA and LAMPCEOPHORIA) - VULCANALIA 23rd August.

HERA: Festivals at Argos in honour of Juno.

HILARIA: 25th March at Rome in honour of Cybele.

HYACINTHIA: In honour of Hyacinthus and Apollo observed at Sparta in July for nine days.

HYDROPHORIA: At Athens in memory of deluge victims, (DEUCALION), also a festival in honour of Apollo.

INOA: In memory of Ino (a sea goddess) in Corinth, Megara and Laconia. Medieval witch-ducking probably originate from her customs.

IOLAIA: In honour of Hercules and Iolas.

ISCHENIA: At Olympia in honour of Ischenus (grandson of Mercury and Hiera)
ISEA: In honour of Isis, nine day event (crop festival)

ISTHMIA: For sea deity Melicerta (Ino's son) in Corinth.

ITHOMAIA: In honour of Jupiter, including musical contests at Ithome.

JUNONALIA and JUNONIA: In honour of Juno, at Rome same as HERA.

LAMPTERIA: In Pallene in Achaia in honour of Bacchus.

LARARIA: In honour of Lares in December, Lares also celebrated in May.

LAURENTALIA: 23rd Dec and 30th April in honour of Laurentia.

LECTISTERNIA: In honour of Neptune, Apollo Diana and others in times of public chaos.

LEMURIA and LEMURALIA: In May, first called REMURIA, to appease the Manes of Remus.

LENOEA: In honour of Bacchus.

LIBERALIA and LIBERIA: 17th March in honour of Bacchus.

LITHOBO'LIA: At Troezene in honour of Limia and Auxesia.

LUCARIA and LUCERIA: At Rome, 1st Feb and or in July.

LUPERCALIA: In honour of Pan in Rome on 15th February.

MAIAMA: 1st May in honour of Maia.

MEDITRINALIA: Festival of Meditrina; 30th Sept - feast of first fruits.

MEGALESIA: 12th April, in honour of Cybele.

MERCURY: A merchant's feast day in this god's honour, 15th May.

METAGITNIA: In honour of Apollo, at Melite.

MINERVALIA: Celebrated in March and June in Rome by scholars.

NEMORALIA: In honour of Diana in Africa.

NEOMENIA: New moon festival to honour 'all' the Gods, especially Apollo and Diana.

NEPHALIA: Greek festival to honour Mnemosyne.

NICETERIA: In memory of Minerva's victory over Neptune.

NUDIPEDALIA: Sacrifices at Lacedmon in times of public calamity.

NUMENIA: See NEOMENIA.

OPICONSIVA: In honour of Vesta, celebrated on the 8th of the Calends of September.

OPALIA: Festivals in honour of the goddess Ops.

ORGIA: Celebration of Bacchus (his triumph in India)

OSCHOPHORIA: Connected with Bacchus (in Athens).

PAGANALIA: Roman feast in honour of Ceres celebrated in January.

PALILIA: In honour of Pales, celebrated on 21st April, (also called the PARILIA).

PAMMILIA: Greek sacrifices.

PAMYLIA: In honour of the nurse of Osiris Pamyle, at Egypt.

PANATHEN'A: For Minerva at Athens, they where held on July 7th (great) and May 5th and 6th (lesser).

PANDIA: Held in Athens in honour of Jupiter. It was established by Pandion.

PANELLENIA: Public festival held by the Greeks.

PELOPEA: In honour of Pelops at Elis.

PELORIA: Festival held by the Thessalians.

PHALLICA: Egyptian festival in honour of Osiris.

PLYNTERIA: Greek celebration in honour of Minerva.

PORTUMNALIA: Held in Rome in honour of Portumnus on the borders of the Tiber. (17th August).

PYTHIA: Games in honour of Apollo, held close to temple at Delphi.

QUIRINALIA: In honour of Romulus, on 13th of Calends of March.

QUINQUATRIA: Roman festival in honour of Minerva, for 5 days starting on March 18th.

REGIFUGIUM and FUGALIA: To celebrate the flight of the Tarquins.
SATURNALIA: December festival in honour of Saturn. Most modern Xmas customs have originated from this feast.

SEPTIMONTIUM: December festival held in Rome.

SIGILLARIA: 2-day celebration held at end of SATURNALIA, when small dolls were offered to Pluto and friends.

SUOVETAURILIA: Roman sacrifices held every 5th year.

TERMINALIA: Held in February in honour of Terminus, the god of boundaries.

THEOXENIA: Greek festival to honour all the Gods.

TITHENIDIA: Festival at Sparta, held in the temple of Diana.

TRICLARIA: In honour of Diana at Ionia.

VENERALIA: April feast in honour of Venus.

VERTUMNALIA: October feast in honour of Vertumnus.

VESTALIA: Roman celebration in honour of VESTA, held on 9th June.

VINALIA: Roman celebration in honour of Jupiter & Venus, (Vinalia of Jupiter held in August). For Venus see VENERALIA.

VULCANALIA: August feast of Vulcan.

XANTHICA: Macedonian celebration held in April.

Appendix 2
Jewels

A jewel in vision and dreams is frequently emblematic of increasing wealth and prosperity, but not always in a materialistic sense. The colour of gems and precious stones is also very relevant to the interpretation of the image. The following brief list, drawing on the ancient divination properties of stones and mineral and metals may be of some assistance:

ADULARIA: Has calming effect on the mental faculties.
AMAZONITE: Good for healing and wealth attracting.
AMBER: Gives protection and help with health problems.
AMETHYST: For tranquillity and aids against intoxication.
APATITE: To absorb bad vibrations and stop gossip.
AQUAMARINE: Peace and meditation with increased health.
AVENTURINE: For good fortune and success.
AZURITE: Mental faculty and meditations.
BLACK AGATE: Absorbs negativity and increases strength.
BERYL: Beneficial for the liver and general health.
CALCITE: Soothing and calming properties.
CARNELIAN: Blood purifier and good for new vitality.
CHALCEDONY: Generally for health and vitality.
CHRYSOCOLLA: Remembrance and loyalty.
CHRYSOLITE: Protection, wealth and happiness.
CITRINE: Health and clear thinking.
COAL: Continuity, protection and good luck.
COPPER: For love and protection against illness.
CORAL: For love attraction and magical workings.
DIAMOND: Clarity of the logical mind and inspiration.
DIORITE: For atonement to the earth's cycles.
EMERALD: Happiness, eye disorders and long life.
FLINT: To protect, inspire and strengthen.
FOSSIL ROCK: Astral travel, lucid dreams, the imagination.
GARNET: For power, strength, energy and satisfaction.
GOLD: Attraction of Solar energy and wealth.
GRANITE: Earthing negative energy and helping the mind.
GYPSUM: Happiness and relief from stress.
HIDDENITE: For awareness and knowledge of the unknown.
IRON: For protection and redirection of force.
JADE: Helps visualisation and the imagination.

JASPER: Spiritual awareness and the psychic process.
KYANITE: Calming and aids with concentration.
LAPIS LAZULI: Improves intellect and spiritual awareness.
LIMESTONE: Improves appreciation of self and natural world.
MARBLE: Attracts peace and tranquillity.
MOLYBDENITE: For help with mental stress and illness.
MOONSTONE: Psychic ability and spiritual strength.
NICCOLITE: Friendships, love and fertility.
ONYX: Mental awareness and clarity.
OPAL: Inspires confidence and protection of the ego.
PEARL: Quells aggression and calms the worried mind.
PISOLITE: Attracts affection from opposite sex.
PLATINUM: Psychic protection and strength.
PYRITE: Solar divinations and awareness of self.
QUARTZ: Inspiration, spiritual awareness and energy.
RUBY: For passion and to invigorate the libido.
SAPPHIRE: Improves intellect and deflects negativity.
SERPENTINE: Increased success and healing associations.
SILVER: Imagination, mystery and the hidden.
SLATE: For remembrance and calmness.
SODALITE: Promotes youth and inner visions.
TIGER'S EYE: For protective and wealth attracting charms.
TIN: Deflects deceit and falsehoods.
TOPAZ: Calms and guards the wearer.
TOURMALINE: Improves sensitivity and energy.
TURQUOISE: Tranquillity, success and intuition.
URANINITE: Strongly radio active-beware.
VESUVIANITE: Friendship, happiness and social affairs.
WOLFRAMITE: Strength and longevity.
ZIRCON: Clarity of mind and inspiration.

Appendix 3
Numbers

ONE: The illuminating sun and daylight; the centre and initiation or start of all things. One is the logical conscious mind and the dawn of spirituality in the human being.

TWO: Two is duality and the balance displayed by male and female and God and Goddess principles. Three cannot be brought to light without one and two.

THREE: The result of growth from the basic foundation blocks of duality. It is the Holy-Trinity expressed in Pagan-lunar terms as waxing, full and waning moon or alternatively, maiden, mother and crone aspects; also the sacred triad of Rome and the universal Triple Goddess in all her glory. Also depicts the stressful (yet creative) conflict arising from the actual clashing together of the first two.

FOUR: The four corners of a square which link to the earth element and the four cardinal points of the compass conjoining with seasonal cycles of nature. A number related to protection.

FIVE: The four elements plus the spirit that penetrates all. As such it is the pentagram sacred to the witches' altar. Five stands for the main senses of man, which allow him to experience existence to the full. Five is also the marked day and vibration of Venus; thus it depicts love, fertility and happiness.

SIX: This represents consolidation and unification through the joining of two three-pointed triangles that in turn create a six-pointed star. Six is the hidden sense that allows one to access the world of mystery, divination and magic.

SEVEN: Seven links to the sum total days of the week and the deities and planetary cycles corresponding thereto. It is thus a symbol of perfect completion through endurance, hardship and sometimes pain.

EIGHT: A sign that represents the equalisation of opposing agents. The serpents rampant on the caduceus of Hermes fight and strain against each other to create eventual harmony, finally accomplished in the image of the figure '8'. It is also a life-sign through the cellular-like mating of two creative twisting circles.

NINE: The triple strength of the Triple Goddess is a symbol of great power and truth. Today, because of its association with emergency services (i.e. 999) this sign represents speedy assistance in the popular human consciousness. Ancient man also needed frequent help, and the Goddess obviously once answered the spiritual necessity for an emergency psychic help-line in times of greatest danger.

TEN: The pentacle doubled is another power sign. The actual duplication of the five-pointed star leads us to a mirror image that results in reflective lunar qualities. Ten, with its nostalgic reflection, brings us back again to the unifying aspects of one. To some, it is a symbol of return, reincarnation and a new state of being.

Appendix 4
Symbols

ABYSS: The underworld, the unknown, the depths of the subconscious mind, fear of things that cannot be seen or understood.

ACCIDENT: Blatant cops and robbers movie and TV images flood through the popular consciousness every night, but may relate to warnings over future short-term travel. Alternatively, it might be warning against taking unwise actions in business enterprises, love affairs etc.

ACROBAT: The symbol of reversal, seeing people or events from another point of view or perspective. The tarot image of the hanged man links with acrobat (reversed man), leading to self-sacrificial imagery.

AEROPLANE: The astral plane, higher levels of consciousness. Escape from problems and worries. Freedom from dictatorship because of the cross-shape, implying sacrifice (this is especially true for Christian-interpreters). The four elements of earth, air, fire and water.

AFFAIR (love): Wishing for the greener grass on the other side of the fence, desire to improve your sexual and emotional connections with others, the need for attention and love, a warning not to lead your life on emotional levels only.

AILMENTS: May portend trouble or an unfavourable result. It may also relate to a damaged ego following an emotional setback. Sometimes means that events will be delayed.

ALBATROSS: It was once believed that these birds, which followed ships, were the souls of lost sailors. Because of this association they are linked to reincarnation and the afterlife. Also a sign of sea voyages to come.

ALCOHOL: The desire to escape from everyday problems and responsibilities. Also, if drinking in company, the need for stimulating companionship or acceptance. May foretell celebrations, weddings etc, to come.

ALLIGATOR: Symbol of the terrors or the unknown, the deep uncharted depths of the reptilian lower-mind – a warning to take care.

ALTAR: Place of spiritual authority, gateway to other dimensions and levels of existence - in simpler terms, place of judgement, liberation and self-sacrifice.

AMETHYST: Mental stability and good fortune to come, satisfaction in all matters of the mind.

AMMUNITION: For a woman, seeing ammunition represents the seed produced and 'fired' by the phallus (which is the gun and bow and weapon of masculinity). To a man, ammunition is the fertilising spermatozoon. If ammunition lies untouched, then can be sign of sterility or sexual frustration, if being fired then depicts the need for sexual satisfaction.

ANTS: Sign of minor troubles worrying the interpreter. Any such creatures that get under your feet in annoying fashion are firm warnings to stop letting unimportant matters clog up your life.

ANVIL: Sign of the Roman fire god Vulcan and the Greek Hephaestus, god of blacksmiths. To see an anvil is a sign of new events to come that will be beneficial.

APE: Sign of betrayal and deceit - beware, someone is not being straight with you. Watch your back or you will be taken for a ride.

APPLE: A of riches and good fortune. They are also frequently seen as a herald of romance and affection. The latter is especially so with rosy red apples.

ARM: A warning that you must sacrifice something dear to progress in your mission. An arm that is cut off denotes financial or emotional loss. Mythologically, an arm denotes strength and compromise as in tales of the Celtic god Nuada and the later Cornish Saint Mylor.

ARMCHAIR: Sign of the desire for peace and contentment. Also denotes family connections with older relatives for obvious reasons.

ARROW: If you are anxiously waiting news of an important event then the arrow is likely to appear before you just prior to its arrival. Check the surrounding symbols to discover if it warns of good or disappointing news.

AUTUMN: The end of the season heralds winter's hardship but it also marks the rich abundance of natural bounty. Because of this, autumn can be either a positive or a negative sign.

AXE: Symbol of strength and dependability - also a sign of starting fresh projects that may prove advantageous to the seer. Change is approaching fast.

BABY: The situation that the baby is seen in reflects the message that needs to be understood. Sick babies denote hardships to be endured, while smiling, happy babes tell us that life is soon to improve.

BARBER: To dream of such a person is a sign of business ventures and change.

BASEMENT: Seeing yourself in this place is a reflection of what is resting in the subconscious mind. Other surrounding images must be heeded to ascertain the nature of the vision and dream. It can be a warning to listen to that little voice (the subconscious) that is trying hard to tell you something of vital importance.

BAT: Symbolic of the unconscious; they belong to the realm of darkness and thus the unknown or feared aspects of self. Often seen as an emblem of death and illness. Much of the bat's bad press is through the negative efforts of the early Church to equate it with evil and the Devil; actually, they are quite charming little fellows really. The Chinese regard bats as signs of happiness and contentment.

BEAR: Symbol of crude unpredictable power, the rampant egotistical side of self that must be sometimes put in its place, also, the primordial giant (maybe the school bully).

BEAVER: Sign of striving hard towards your ambition without much rest. Also may be seen as symbol of overcoming problems that seems larger than you. Although usually a peaceful animal, beavers are strong and certainly not afraid to attack big carnivores that try to eat them.

BED: Much depends on what context the bed is seen in, for a young agile person a sign of sexual progress or alternatively the need for rest from physical exertion, for the elderly, a sign again of rest and contentment or sometimes illness. On deeper levels, the bed denotes the secure nature of a mother's womb and the solitude found therein.

BEE: Organisation, industrious action, advancement and creative productivity. This is a very ancient Pagan emblem of working towards your aspirations.

BEETLES: Symbolic of minor irritations and family trouble.

BELLS: May be heard in festive note or alternatively gloomy in nature. Happy bells denote weddings and good news arriving soon. Tenebrous chimes herald loss, defeat, illness and hardships (even funerals) on the horizon.

BIRTH: Visions and dreams of birth may remain largely insignificant for pregnant women, where they may be expected. To have such visions at other periods of your life is another matter altogether. The concept of birth is emblematic of new beginnings and happy events that may be totally unconnected with actual physical birth. Symbolically birth marks a time of transformation, a time when energies take on new form. For a man in a hostile environment it may depict a subconscious desire to return to the warm safety of the mother's womb. For a woman it may represent the desire (or fear) of pregnancy. Generally, birth dreams precede happy events and changes for the better in your fortunes.

BLACKBERRIES: Visions of berries or seeds are strongly connected to new ideas and growth. The matter of whether the idea is good or bad depends on the species in question. Although edible, blackberries' dark coloration links them to night, darkness and the negative principle. Traditionally they were often seen as an unlucky sign; however they were also used in protective charms when gathered during the correct phase of the lunar cycle.

BLACKSMITH: Sign of persistence against overwhelming odds. If you see him in dreams then your ambitions will eventually be realized, albeit with much hard labour. The value of the smith was fully appreciated by our pre-Christian Celtic ancestors. Goibniu was the patron deity of this trade. The Tuatha De Danann ('People of the Goddess Danu') relied on him to craft weapons to combat their sworn enemy the Fomorians. Because of this ancient traditional link, we may also view the smith as a possible omen of trouble to come that we must prepare for. Be on your guard, be ready and don't get caught out is the message from this sign.

BLOOD: The universal symbol of life and sacrifice. The sight of blood causes many people to collapse when their blood pressure drops and unconsciousness comes to save them from further distress. Blood can also cause panic and fear in numerous people, which again is a perfectly natural human survival reaction. Symbolically, blood is linked to new life and hope for a better future. The modern Christian sacrificial aspect of blood is nothing new. Many Pagan deities and their myths connect to this current of thought process. Blood links us to the concept of resurrection, reincarnation and rebirth.
BLUEBIRD: Sign of luxury, youth and happy occasions.

BOAR: Because of its 'head-down and charge' mentality, the Boar stands as a sign of wild, unthinking bravado. To see it in dreams is a warning to look before you leap. You may be about to embark upon an unwise course of events in your life, so check out your plans from all angles before it's too late.

BOAT: Anything that floats on the water is directly or indirectly connected with the mental faculty. To travel upon light seas denotes pleasant events forthcoming. Voyages in stormy waters are an omen of worries and troubles to come. To be flung into heavy turbulent seas from a boat is a warning to be aware of illness and mental problems.

BOLT: A sign of obstacles in your progress through life, it can be a warning to liberate yourself from everyday drudgery and boredom especially if the bolt appears in a recurring dream.

BOMB: Symbol of pent-up rage (or fear) and suppressed emotions. Because of the explosive aspect this vision is also strongly connected to sexual ejaculation and especially repressed sexuality. The dynamic principles of the bomb make it particularly significant in an adolescent and teenage (wet) dream state.

BONE: A sign of what rests behind the superficial egocentric self. To strip away the outer layers of the skin and expose the bones is to look within toward many hidden (maybe suppressed) aspects of yourself. In essence, bones subconsciously denote the naked man and woman as nature intended them without the indoctrinated falsehoods of a materialistic society.

BOOK: Books are linked to wisdom, intelligence, harmony and good fortune. They denote periods of calm that are necessary to combat everyday strains and stresses. Books in vision can be a sign from the gods to start a fresh, more beneficial lifestyle. Books are emblematic of spiritual prowess and the power to defeat evil. They are also a symbol of divine secrets that are known to the select few; in ancient times, priests, being the only people who could read holy writ, would hold the spiritual monopoly over the populace. Wisdom always has a price; it's up to us to discover if this price is worth paying. "Avoid the stress and enjoy life with less." That has to be the sensible watchword here.

BOOT: Because of its connection with the earth the boot and shoe sign is linked to travel. To see an old worn out boot is symbolic of stagnation, lethargy and depression in your life. A new shiny boot denotes vitality and happy journeys to follow quite soon.

BOW: To draw a bow and to loose an arrow is subconsciously linked to casting a thought or emotion into the uncertainties of life. The great god Apollo destroyed the serpent Python with his bow and arrow. The serpent had been sent by the goddess Juno to persecute Latona (Apollo's mother). The bow often features in mythology as an instrument of justice and vengeance, most notable in popular consciousness as in the (quite recent) Robin Hood legend for instance. It can also be seen today as a symbol of righting wrongs or putting old scores to rest. The bow is also symbolic of being love-struck as with Cupid's Arrows of passion.

BOX: Symbolically, a compartmentalization of the mind. Whatever one discovers inside the box is what dwells within the deepest part of the human consciousness. Hopes and fears are all possible in the mysterious confines of the box. The obvious aspect of containment makes the box a feminine sign, containment in this instance relating to the genital and sexual act, but also to burial. These aspects of the box link first to life (i.e.-sexuality and containment) and secondly to death as in coffin and burial i.e. returning to the Goddess and Mother Earth. The box then represents the hidden face lurking under the ordinary, everyday persona.

BRANCH: Linked to all aspects concerning trees. Branches that appear windswept or broken are bad omens. To see branches bearing lush foliage or fruits is a very good sign of future prosperity.

BREAD: Good wholesome bread is a sign of family harmony and togetherness. The pragmatic Romans even had a goddess called Fornax who was given the task of presiding over the baking of bread. Visions of mouldy inedible bread are a harbinger of misfortune, illness and poverty.

BREWING: To dream of brewing wine or beer is a good sign. Brewing and merriment often go hand in hand. The Roman god of wine was Bacchus and during his festivals the revellers would experience great fun and games. Such beverages have ancient sacrificial and religious associations. The contemporary Wiccan rite of "Cakes and Ale" and the Christian Transubstantiation of wine into the blood of Christ are the most recent examples of this mystical process. The sacrificial aspect of these fluids can be traced back into ancient mythology. For more on this subject see the above comments on blood.

BRICKS: Bricks are used to make walls, thus they are a sign of subconscious barriers and taboos. They are also connected with building shelters to house people so alternatively they may denote growth and increased finances. It is important to take careful note of surrounding signs when seeking to decipher such a seemingly contradictory symbol as this. To see bricks being smashed is symbolic of personal liberation from oppression and the freedom of spirit.

BRIDE: A wedding featuring a beautiful happy bride is a grand omen. To see one in rags is a sign of misery and hardship. We can find links to the term 'bride' in the ancient Celtic goddess Brigit, who was also known as Brighid and Bride. This potent Gaelic deity was to be later canonized into Saint Bridget (450-523) by crafty missionaries in Kildare, Ireland.

BRIDGE: Symbol of change from one state and place and level or emotion to another. Seeing a bridge in vision and dream, especially after a dispute, denotes the desire to repair the rift, hence the term 'building bridges'. Bridges are often places of danger and one has to brave in order to get to a safer place or level of understanding. The act of taking-on that bridge can result in the death of the old, materialistic self as higher intelligence is gained. To cross a bridge with ease portends good fortune. Troublesome crossings foretoken disaster and ruination.

BROOM: A very old Pagan sign of love and prosperity. Christianity deviously created the mediaeval, ugly witch hag on a broomstick stereotype image. The origins for this cruel vilification probably arose from old fertility rites when villagers would sing and dance around the growing young spring crops. Part of the celebrations involved jumping to the height of a brush in hope that the local genius and spirit of the corn would allow the harvest to grow to a similarly impressive height. The old Pagan hand-fasting (wedding) ceremony sometimes involved the happy couple leaping over a birch brush; obviously the puritanical Christians of the period saw this as sexually immoral which led to further denigration of native folklore, symbolism and customs. To see visions of sweeping with a new broom denotes increasing benefit in finances or romance.

BROTHER: To a man this is a sign of competition and challenge. To a woman it is symbolic of companionship and helpfulness. Naturally, such a sign as this is wide open to personal interpretation, depending solely upon the family relationship of the subject in question.

BUBBLES: These can be a warning against being misused by others in whom we trust. Bubbles form a connection between the realms of visible and the invisible thus they depict magic and the unknown. They link together the elements of water and air and finalise them by exploding into pure, unadulterated spirit. This symbol tells one to beware of fairy favours that are like glory - little more than fleeting.

BUGS: Commonly seen as a sign of minor irritation or worry, however also a symbol of industrious activity and creative energy. This is especially so if the image is of an insect displaying social interconnections with others i.e. ants, termites, bees, wasps etc. The two latter signs can obviously (because of their nature) be warnings of ill health and arguments.

BUILDINGS. We subconsciously see dwelling places as extensions of our deeper self. To view a ramshackle house in vision is to see aspects of our innermost nature that we would rather keep hidden, i.e. feelings of guilt, depression, fear or anxiety. Buildings that appear clean and luxurious reflect feelings (or plans) of joy, peace and contentment.

BULL: The horns of the bull are a strong lunar symbol. Many cultures held this animal in high esteem as a sign of various atmospheric deities. To some it was lunar, others had it as a mark of the Thunder God, whilst to the Romans it was the Sun-Bull of the solar and war-god Mithras. It represents the (masculine) fertilising shafts of sunlight that bring new life to the waiting (feminine) earth. It is suggestive of strong male sexuality or libido that can become obsessively all embracing i.e. rage. Thus the Bull is quite a complex emblem, much more than just "a bull in a china-shop".

BURIAL: Like the death card in the Major Arcana, this sign is not always as negative as it first appears. Burial is a return to the safety of Mother Earth, she who nourishes and protects us from harm. It is a sign of change; when one cycle ends another new one begins. This is sometimes symbolic of a deeper desire to leave the material world behind in order to mould your being into greater heights of achievement.

BURNING: The creative divine spark that dwells within us all is often seen as fire. Fire destroys but in its destruction it also creates anew. Materialistically, see it as a sign of increasing fortunes and energy. Spiritually, view it as the purifying light that connects us to the realm of the gods, the desire to become a better, nobler person. Horrific dreams of burning may result from a troubled or guilty conscience especially if the dream or vision is persistently recurring. Alternatively, it could be suggestive of death or injury in a previous incarnation.

CAGE: The actual cage is within the viewer. To be trapped therein is a sign of frustration and anxiety. To break free is to liberate yourself from oppression and hardship, either created from communication with other people and circumstances or solely by your own misplaced efforts. The first thing to do if cages appear in vision is to relax and closely scrutinise your situation for faults. The gods can only warn; we must provide the ears to listen and the eyes to see.

CAKE: A very good sign of happy events to come. The cake is the effort of labour and ingredients necessary to create harmony; as such it foretells beneficent relationships and fair balance in life, a great time for new projects to begin.

CALL: To hear your name distantly shouted (even though the caller isn't really there) in the small hours, often suddenly jerks you into fully waking consciousness. A similar event arises when we have a nightmare about falling down stairs. We wake up in a cold sweat, thankful that we are not actually harmed in any fashion. This type of dream is typical of the mind changing its focus from the mundane level to the world of vision and fantasy. The everyday mind is resisting its journey into the nether-world, just like a reluctant dental patient fighting off the effects of anaesthetic gas. The mind can be extremely conservative, not wishing to change from one level of focus to another. The call then, is a panic button, which arises from a highly active mental level, unwilling to change into a lower gear. If the caller is seen and known then it may be a warning to beware of danger approaching soon. If it comes from a known deceased person, then regard it as possible direction from the spirit world and analyse your situation with care.

CAMEL: This odd creature is emblematic of the conscious mind. This is because the camel is a beast of the hot regions blessed (and sometimes damned) by the sun. The sun is of the conscious light of day aspect, whereas the moon depicts the deeper subconscious levels of night. The camel is a good sign; it is the animal that represents hope and survival in hostile environments.

CAMERA: On the materialistic level this is a token warning that someone in whom you trust is not as sincere as they may have first appeared. This is especially so if it is they who point the camera at you. You are being scrutinised in a cold, uncaring manner and your subconscious is telling you this fact very clearly indeed. On deeper astral levels the camera is a symbol of your consciousness. We use the lenses as we use our conscious focus, zooming from one subject (awareness) to another. The camera then is a vehicle that allows us, in vision and dreams, to shift from one place to another in the fastest possible time.

CANAL: Water of any kind links with the subconscious mind and canals are no exception. Peaceful canals surrounded in natural beauty are representative of inner peace or at least the wish for such a blessing, whilst derelict canals that are grey and polluted herald poverty and illness. The latter is a sure warning to change direction in life or face the uncomfortable consequences soon to be experienced.

CANDLE: The light in the darkness and thus illumination of spirit. The flickering flame of a candle is virtually timeless. It depicts the divine spark in us all, the power of creation in which we all inherently share. An unlit candle stands for disappointment and delay; the flame that is absent means powerlessness and the inability to venture into wished-for places on many levels.

CANE: To some the cane is a symbol of authority and discipline, especially those persons who see (or saw) fit to use it to inflict pain on their minions. Obviously to the receiver it is symbolic of brutality, harsh authority and the abuse of power. It also stands for religious intolerance against minorities.

CASTLE: The fortress that contains treasure is symbolic of hidden mysteries. The castle depicts that which may sometimes be feared, but which also holds a curiously mystical attraction. It is the gateway to other worlds that lie beyond the known levels of consciousness.

CAT: Cats in dreams are frequently warnings of dangers to come. Because of their magical associations, they are symbolic of the instinctive self. Black cats are often linked to the negative, rather than positive, aspects of life such as death and destruction. Many cats together are a warning to beware of attacks from enemies, being scratched by a friendly cat heralds deceitful action against you by family or acquaintances. The sound of a cat mewing denotes people you trust telling falsehoods behind your back - time to beware. The cat is the creature that links us to the silent levels of the deep self. Without doubt, dangers may come with the sign of the cat but wisdom is also closely related to this animal; to see it as a purely negative emblem is short-sighted.

CATERPILLAR: Very symbolic of childhood. Small things that fascinate the immature mind sometimes get forgotten, but never quite completely. Caterpillars hold the secret of transformation from one state of being to another. They tell us to prepare ourselves for big changes to come.

CATHEDRAL: To the monotheist, these vast structures stand for high ideals and spiritual grandeur. To those of a pantheistic worldview, cathedrals are often temples of suppression of native culture and the repression of indigenous races. What is sacred to one is profane to another and vice-versa.

CAVE: The home of the unknown, the place where we face our inner fears and conflicts. Dark foreboding caves are (like castles) gateways to other interior and exterior dimensions.

CEMETERIES: On the physical level we perceive cemeteries as places of sadness, loss and remembrance. Death however in all his gloomy countenance is to the deeper mind not quite that simple. Death is not an end it is an adventure. We are an important composite aspect of the spiritual whole of creation and creative energy. This energy (the divine spark) that propels us is not destroyed at the time of death. Although we leave behind our physical frame we liberate that force which we call in our ignorance the spirit. Just as a tadpole sheds its old self to transform into the frog, we too must return back to the cosmic source in order to be improved and reborn again into the next vital incarnation. In the untrained person this knowledge seems often to be lacking especially in his and her conscious worldview. However the subconscious mind of even the most materialistic type of person usually realises more than we give it credit for. The deeper mind knows and tells us that visions of death and cemeteries are omens of change which are not necessarily always connected with actual physical death. They can be signs that your life is about to change drastically. They frequently herald the end of one phase and commencement of another, which may be beneficial.

CHAFFINCH: This bird may be common but its lovely song matched with its beautiful plumage is a joy to behold, a symbol of fine times and happy holidays.

CHAINS: All the life-problems that we perceive as mental burdens can manifest on the astral level as chains of one sort or another. We usually allow this negative state of affairs to come into existence by our own wrong thinking. At times we are all guilty of this no matter how spiritually mature we may be. Chains are symbols of oppression that is often self-inflicted, although outside influences may bring subjugation and pessimism to an otherwise optimistic person. If you see chains in dreams then it is time to examine with care your own perception of the world about you.

CHALICE: The cup of emotion and spiritual enlightenment. Chalices and goblets abound in myth and legend, one of the most recent being the Holy Grail of Arthurian fame. The semi-mythical King Arthur story became a Norman romancer's Christianization of much older Pagan tales of the Old Gods. We have already spoken of the link between cups, hearts and love. When we see this sign in vision we may be receiving a message from the gods telling us that life is soon to take on a greater degree of spirituality. The chalice is, for a younger person, an important herald of love and desire for fulfilment. The more mature individual may see it as a symbol of the higher self that seeks to link us to divinity. This is the greater spiritual awareness or intelligence that dwells deep within us all, what the ancient Romans knew intimately as the 'genius.'

CHAMELEON: The creature of change. Its well known trait of altering its skin colour to match backgrounds gives us a strong clue to just why and how the subconscious mind uses it in symbolic communication. It stands as an emblem of deceit and mistrust. What cannot be seen perceived or understood is usually not something in that the layman believes he can trust. The chameleon is then the quintessential warning of the turncoat in our midst. We should view it as a sign that all is not as it first appears.

CHARIOT: Symbolic of war gods like Mars and Ares. This is a dynamic sign that life is about to take on greater momentum, possibly for the better.

CHESS: The dualistic mind and the fight between light and dark and good against evil. A battle in your life.

CHICKENS: Frequently seen as a sign of minor troubles. Although chickens are winged creatures they have (because of their reluctance to fly) strong associations with the earth element. Their habit of scratching the ground for food is connected to annoying little problems that plague the mind.

CHIMNEY: Long tapering chimneys may be phallic symbols suggesting that the dream and vision be connected to sexuality. On deeper planes they can also be firm signs of religiosity, solid materialistic structures reaching upward to penetrate the heavens, thus connecting man with the Gods. It's good sign in general.

CIRCLE: A symbol of eternity, infinity and the sacred Goddess and God. Our earliest folk memories stem from distant times when mankind held that great life-giver the sun in highest esteem. The moon too, that sign of the lunar goddess in her full glory, has a long history in our psychic development as a species on this planet. (Incidentally, Kitanitowit the supreme god of the Algonquin Indians is often represented as a full circle because he represents the whole world and everything in it.) The solar, lunar and planetary aspects remind us of the complete circle. The circle is one of the strongest life signs we possess and to see it in vision and meditation is a very firm herald of increased vitality, dynamism and optimism. The circle really has no beginning or end. It marks a constant flow of force and energy that can be changed but never actually destroyed.

CITY: To see a busy city where everything is grimy and chaotic is a sign of mental torpor, indecision and anxiety. To see a city as shiny, new and flourishing bodes well for future business and social enterprises that one may be planning.

CLOCK: Our earliest markers of time were the sun and the moon, four weeks being one month or *'moonth'* as it should be correctly called. The sign of the clock is a sign of waiting. It is only natural for man to want power over time but in many ways this remains an insurmountable obstacle. Time is like physical death because it is something that we cannot defeat. The clock then is symbolic of our hopes and fears over life and death. The ancient Roman god Janus was usually portrayed with two heads facing opposite directions. One looked to the future whilst the other marked the past. Janus, as a keeper of sacred time, holds the key to many questions including those connected with time.

CLOUDS: Dark foreboding clouds are signs of trouble and hardship whilst blue sky and high white cloud is a good herald of imminent prosperity after stern challenges.

COAT: Protection and all aspects relating to it. The coat is a layer that shields us from the elements. In dreamtime it represents a defence against whatever is threatening the dreamer. To lose a coat is to fear loss of a part of your personality or character. If a friend or relative loses their coat this denotes trouble or illness for that particular person, torn coats mean that hardship, despair and strife are close at hand, time to strengthen your defences.

COCKEREL: The quintessence of what his name logically implies i.e. cockiness. It's a symbol of proud arrogance, a warning to not rely solely on your ego for progression through life.

COIN: In mundane terms, symbolic of material wealth. However coins hold more mystery on the initiated levels than we may at first realise. Gold coins stand for the solar orb and the logical and conscious physical world, whilst silver ones depict the feminine and intuitive level connected with magic and the moon. Brass or copper coloured coins connect with the earth and lower planes of existence.

COMET: A glorious sign of revelation and inspiration. The comet is divine spiritual power manifesting on the physical plane. There is, however, a more sinister side to this vision. In history, comets have often been seen as harbingers of doom and disaster. In April 1066 the appearance of Halley's Comet in the night's sky filled the common folk with dread and prophecies of evil were given by the wise. England's sorry fate at the hands of the victorious Normans later that year and the radical suppression of Saxon life is now well known. Certainly makes you think doesn't it?

COMPASS: To see a spinning needle in a compass is representative of anxiety and indecision. A steady compass means that the right answer to pressing questions will soon be found.

COPPER: This metal whilst beautiful is somewhat inferior to gold. It is the tarnished face of the sun and as such belongs to the lower levels of existence. In occult terms copper has associations with the great goddess Venus and all things connected to love and lust and beauty. Copper then is a sign of the sexual nature of things and this is especially true in a young person's dream and vision.

CORK: A strong and popular sign of celebration and family joys. Expect news of weddings or births to come into your realm quite soon. Corks floating on top of water mark your struggle in life to challenge adversity.

CORN: To be involved in the harvest denotes friendship and happy events to come. Running corn through your fingers is a sign of financial success and inheritance. Running in golden fields of corn is symbolic of total liberation from the heavy shackles of mundane, worldly problems.

CORPSE: Symbolic of unhappy events to come and general pessimism. This is a warning to be on your guard against wrongdoers and criminals. It is also a warning to watch out for minor health problems that may escalate into major troubles. Like the sign of death in the Tarot, it can sometimes herald important changes in life, which may eventually (after a struggle) be for the better.

COW: Sign of the winter turning into the warm abundance of summer, also a symbol of kind, maternal instincts and care. The cow has lunar, air and earth associations. The Egyptian goddess Hathor was frequently portrayed in the guise of a cow. The great Isis also frequently sported cow's horns upon her head, although this link probably owes much to her amalgamation with Hathor. This gentle creature was often revered then as a spiritual sign of the great Mother Goddess of the universe. This is a far cry from today as the cow is now treated as nothing more than a milk-producing machine to be exploited for business profit. She is artificially inseminated, robbed of her calf when it is but days old and finally killed young as a worn out milker to make frequently unwholesome burgers. Many will associate this sign with pregnancy and maternal instinct. However, to a committed Vegan (one who abstains from consuming animal products including eggs and milk), the cow stands as a prime totem of man's greed and destruction of Mother-Earth.

CRANE: Symbolic of the desire for independence and liberty.

CROCODILE: To see the vision of this creature is to be warned in a very sure manner indeed. Do not trust anyone who appears to be connected with this image for to do so is to court bad fortune and disaster. Animals that crawl out of dark waters in a dangerous fashion represent the negative aspects of self, secretly lurking in the hidden pools of the deep, subconscious mind.

CROSS: A sacrificial sign for obvious reasons, also representative of punishment, death and humiliation. A balanced, four-armed cross denotes equilibrium whilst one with unequal arms marks a period of discord and unease. Incidentally, this old truth is well represented in the equal and unequal crosses (Gyfu & Nyd) of the Runic Futhork. To a traveller it may be symbolic of decisions that must be made. It's also a sign of direction with its four-quarter points on the compass.

CROW: This bird has many links to the ancient Celtic goddess of battle and death, the Morrigan and Morrigu. This isn't surprising when we remember that the hoodie-crow would have enjoyed rich pickings on old battlefield sites, following the gross carnage. The Crow's dark colour also links it with night and all things therein, a rather negative symbol that warns one to be extremely vigilant.

DABCHICK: This little bird denotes security and continuity. Anyone who has ever watched this amusing bird skulking about in the reeds will understand his persistent nature and realise how easily he relates to your own particular situation. A good sign for sure.

DAGGER: Be wise in your choice of friends for one may not be as trustworthy as you first believed. Daggers, swords and knives link with the element of air, although some prefer to join them to the realm of fire.

DANCE: Sign of freedom from oppression and of the liberation of the true self, also a token of celebrations and increasing sexuality, especially in younger persons.

DARKNESS: To see naught but the dark can warn of ill times ahead, but we need to remember that without the dark there can be no light. Without chaos there can never be absolute harmony. Everything has its opposite and we must remain philosophical in this sure knowledge. Like they say, "every cloud has its silver lining," although at a bad time this may be of little consolation.

DEATH: To dream of a long dead person may foreshadow an important event. This spirit has come to offer us help. It is our free choice whether or not we wish to accept it. The mind still retains much of its everyday logic in dreams, however to understand this logic we must remember that symbolism is the name of the game in dreamtime. Thus any questions we may have answered by a spirit will probably be conveyed as signs. To dream that one is dead marks a strong desire to escape mundane reality and problems. Death may not come as an end but as a whole new beginning. It stands for changing energies on all levels of existence.

DESERT: Hardships and strife are near when we see this vision. The desert destroys moisture leaving only arid wasteland. The wasteland in question may be your deep self that is longing for some type of assistance and support from life-troubles. A change of career might be the answer here. Excessive sun kills on the desert, so overindulgence as a causative factor might be suggested by the subconscious in this vision. Avoidance of overdoing things is indicated.

DIAMOND: This is often a very good sign that events are soon to improve quite dramatically on the physical plane, for more insight on this interesting symbol see 'Cards'.

DIVE: To dive into clear blue water portends a happy state of affairs ahead, especially on the mental level. To enter dark foreboding water augurs a decline in your welfare. The most important thing to remember is that water usually represents an aspect of the deeper mind. The everyday consciousness (the diver) plunges into the water (subconscious levels) so the actual state and clarity of the water directly relates to the mental harmony and balance of the dreamer.

DOG: Multi-complex symbol. Happy dogs denote loyalty and friendships. Fighting, snarling dogs warn of enemies in our midst. Legendary black dogs have often appeared to warn people before disasters occur. The mythical three-headed dog Cerberus is the guardian of Pluto's Kingdom. He reminds us of the dog's role as faithful servant unto death. Cerberus, with his triple-head aspect, becomes a type of dreaded Holy-Trinity. He is friend ally to the righteous. Alternatively, he is monster, fiend and devourer to the wicked. Baying, lonely dogs herald, like the Banshee, death, sadness and separation. Although, as we have seen, the dog is frequently associated with death, its vital symbolism is essentially good and positive. The author often has visitations in dreamtime from his loyal black dog Midge who left the physical dimension some time ago. Midge usually gives warning that danger or error is close at hand. He also helps to find lost items. The dog is never to be underestimated. His intimate connection and loyalty to mankind stretches far back into pre-history. His staunch faithfulness to us bridges many barriers, even death itself. The wise will accept this image as a true gift from the Old Gods; these images are, I believe, often the visiting spirits of our loyal canine pals. Ignore them at your peril.

DONKEY: Mules, donkeys and asses are, because of their sometimes-contentious nature, the epitome of stubbornness. As a beast of burden, this animal represents slow but sure progress with delays along the way. Loud aggressive braying is a mark of the fool, laughing behind your back. To dream of one is a sign that the individual should look to higher things instead of getting bogged down with business affairs and the like - time for a holiday?

DOOR: A sign of journeys to other places. These places may be not of the physical world but the spiritual. To step through a doorway into a darkened room is symbolic of entering the deeper mind. What we find in the room gives us a clue to whatever problems the subconscious is directing our attentions to. We ignore these signs at our peril particularly if the vision and dream is recurring. A door that cannot be opened is symbolic of hidden problems and anxiety.

DRUM: An important event in your life is soon to take place. The question is whether or not the dreamer is capable of facing it.

DUCK: It is unwise to generalise on this family because of its vast diversity but ducks are commonly given to denote travel across water. They also represent finery and the need to impress acquaintances. Drab ducks stand for disappointment and low self-esteem. Ducks with beautiful coloured plumage are a sign of inflated egos and fat-cat luxury.

DWARF: To see other persons surrounding you in the form of dwarves mark delusions of grandeur and feelings of superiority. If the vision shows you as a dwarf amongst giants then the reverse is the case.

EAGLE: The bird of Jupiter (Iuppiter) king of the Roman gods. The grace and majestic power displayed by the eagle is emblematic of the spiritual principal and warm light of day. It is the creature of the Sun and denotes understanding overcoming the dark powers of chaos. It is the ultimate symbol of victory and conquest over lower forces. It's not surprising that the Roman legions held the eagle banner high in front of their advancing battalions at every opportunity.

EARS: Some disrespectful individual is spreading malicious gossip behind your back. Ears are flapping at your expense thus you need to find out who the culprit is quickly. Beware of jealous spies amongst your associates.

EARTHQUAKE: Warning of momentous events soon to occur in your life. It may also relate to worldwide strife and aggression. Without wishing to sound overtly pessimistic, this sign is not one to be taken lightly. Health should be given high priority following this dangerous vision.

EGG: Portends new beginnings, money and fresh opportunities arising soon. Also denotes birth for obvious reasons. To fry eggs is to play with (hatch) vital new ideas. To see broken and rotten eggs is to lose temporary control of a tricky situation. May also denote need for security.

ELEPHANT: Sign of great wealth and good fortune. To ride an Elephant is to rise highly above lesser mortals. Even the tiger trembles before a man on this lofty height. If this symbol appears before us in any form then business, financial, matrimonial and other affairs bode well.

ENGINE: The engine is analogous with the vital life-essence within man. Fast engines denote busy life-styles and hectic events ahead. Sluggish engines herald boredom and ill-health and lost opportunities, although slow engines sometimes link with tranquillity and contentment.

EYE: Like the ears, this is a warning to beware of deceitful actions from others. Someone who certainly does not have your best interests at heart is watching you. In a lighter vein, eyes can suggest that an admirer is hoping to catch your attention even though you have not consciously realised this fact just but.

FAIRY: A multi-functional symbol of our rich Pagan culture and heritage. In a layman's terminology the 'wee good folk' are generally a beneficent sign.

FALCON: Sign of the hunter. To see a falcon is to take control of your affairs and do great deeds, sometimes at the expense of others. It's also symbolic of liberty and freedom.

FALLING: Often when we first enter sleep the active conscious mind resists the pull of slower deeper realms by jerking us out of our slumber with situations involving falling (i.e. off cliffs and buildings stairs etc). Also portends a downward spiral in your business and social dealings.

FATNESS: Traditionally given as a sign of wealth and plenty but in today's more affluent society, fatness can be an emblem for sloth, greed and apathy.

FENCE: A barrier that stands in your way to higher goals. To break down a fence and walk through is to overcome life obstacles. To trip over and into one denotes accidents and mishaps ahead. Fences are walls standing in your way - break them down and move on.

FIELD: The actual state of the field and what is growing in it (if anything) gives the clue to the dream or vision. Lush green pastures denote contentment and easier times to come, whilst black fields of war and destruction forewarn us of strife and misery. The field is like the sea - often analogous with the subconscious mind and everything dwelling within.

FIRE: This element must be respected for danger is never far from its grasp. Fire can be a beneficent vision representing great passion, energy and new growth. Fire is essential to our existence (like all the other elements) for without its vigorous force to stir our emotions we would be much lesser creatures. We should always pay it deep honours and never take it for granted on any level of existence.

FISHHOOK: A chance opportunity is coming your way, which you would be foolish to ignore. Don't let it slip away or you will have to live with the consequences. The gods can be critical and sometimes refuse us a second bite of the cherry.

FLAMINGO: This bird suggests safety in numbers, also the necessity to implement and adapt a new routine for the benefit of your own development on spiritual levels. The flamboyant plumage denotes prosperity.

FLOWER: A multi-complex subject which is beyond the scope of any small list. Generally speaking flowers are emblematic of growth and prosperity. However colour plays an important role in identifying their meaning. Red flowers are for passion and sexual love, whilst black ones are for negativity and sorrow. Blue flowers denote intellect and logical mind. White blossom stands for purity, virginity, the new spring and but sometimes mellow sadness too.

FLYING: Liberation, freedom from oppression, hopes for better times and joy. Flight brings to mind all these feelings, and such a vision may be evidence of the need to open up your true self to a greater, more spiritual life-style. Flight can also be experienced in astral travel. As a child I had many beautiful visions and dreams of flying high over local buildings and trees etc. I believe now that the wonderful aerial sights that I saw were actual (involuntary) journeys of my astral body that had left the physical behind.

FORTRESS: A large impenetrable fort that cannot be breached is symbolic of increasing problems and major worries in security. To be in a fortress overlooking other mortals shows delusions of grandeur and frequently gives evidence of an inferiority complex in the making. The latter may seem a strange, even contrary suggestion at first. Surely, you may ask, standing over others in dominance is a sign of victory and power? That may be so at face value, however those who feel a strong need to dominate their fellows are but spiritual children with all the same hidden insecurities within. The wise person does not compete.

FOX: The old cartoon stereotype of the sly old fox isn't far from the truth - he denotes deceit, theft, risk and malpractice. The fox was frequently seen throughout mediaeval Christian Europe as a sign of Satan. Although Pagans do not believe in a devil figure, the negative concepts of this symbol should be heeded well.

FROG: A sign of childhood and the summer, also emblematic of transformation. The old fairy tale of the frog changing into the handsome prince is ancient evidence of the animal's shape shifting abilities. What child hasn't looked on in awe as the spawn converts into a tadpole which in turn transforms into the frog? The frog marks the transition of elements, especially water into earth. It reminds us of our own evolution from the primordial seas and also our inescapable link to the waters of our mother's womb. To generalise, this is a positive symbol that represents our evolving pathway through life. The situation of the frog in dreams (i.e. good or bad) tells the interpreter whether or not events are boding favourably or otherwise for the future.

FROST: Beautiful, alluring and full of wonderment, but at the same time holding the threat of danger and mishap. "Wrap up warm so that Jack-Frost can't get at you," are familiar words to every small child facing the cold winter's journey to school. I remember seeing the serious look descend on my young niece's face when told this by her granny. A mixture of excitement tempered with thoughtful apprehension set in, which epitomised this sign's message very accurately indeed. The runic symbol for ice is called '*Isa*' or '*Is*' (the latter being Anglo-Saxon) and it portrays the energy of frost. Admire its charm by all means, but beware the dangers lurking within. One slip and all that glistening beauty may seem suddenly less that perfect. In a nutshell, look to your health and take precautions. Isn't life strange? I actually sneezed twice as I wrote this very line; it's a frosty day too.

FUR: Here's another sign which, like human 'obesity', is going through a cultural revolution. Traditionally symbolic of affluence and gross materialistic luxury, the mink coat was once the status mark of every aspirant film star. Now, thanks to the proliferation of anti-fur animal rights organisations in society, fur has become emblematic of greed, cruelty and selfishness. Naturally, our values change. Once it was essential for man to gather fur from animal corpses to survive the cold months, but today it is not necessary. There are now many better man-made materials readily available. Fur is on one hand a symbol of our Neolithic past which evolved into quite recent times as a mark of power and wealth. On the other hand it is now a token sign of avarice and one-upmanship. Possibly a warning from the gods to stop being egotistical and consider others. If you don't you could regret it.

GALE: Sign of a troubled mind. To be blown away is to lose control of the situation, time for a major re-think regarding business, financial and social affairs.

GANNET: Sign of overindulgent greed. The way that gannets launch their attacks on schools of small fish is emblematic of persecution and vilification. It's a symbol to be aware of assaults from above. Maybe your career or business isn't quite as secure as you thought it to be?

GARDEN: A place of great harmony and contentment. To see one in dreams is a good omen for future happiness and fulfilment.

GAZELLE: This lovely little creature has the honour of usually being portrayed in the role of victim. This isn't at all surprising when we remember that gazelles form a substantial part of the diet of large carnivores such as lions. To see a gazelle on astral levels can be a warning to beware. You may become a victim yourself if you are not careful - also a sign to be wary of persecutions from enemies that lurk close by. The old maxim "look before you leap" rings true in this case. Its habit of jumping has been compared to the soul's quest for perfection on the swings, slides and roundabouts of the eternal cosmic dance that we call life.

GHOST: To see an apparition in vision is often a warning to tread carefully for danger is at hand. This is especially so if the spectre is known to you as a lost relative or friend.

GIRAFFE: Symbol of attaining goals that seem to be out of reach - going beyond the normal to achieve the desires that have eluded one for a long time.

GLOVES: This image denotes the need for protection and care. It also warns us not to be cajoled into foolish situations by extrovert time-wasters and gossips. It can also denote a serious challenge to your self-esteem.

GOAT: Because of over a thousand years of monotheistic misrepresentation, the goat has been cast as a sign of evil. This creature is actually symbolic of masculine, fertilising (God-Force) aspects in nature that are crucial for new life and evolution. To see it in dreamtime often relates to the individual's own libido. The image of Old Horny is a very powerful sign of the ancient Horned-God of all nature. His name changes throughout history and within cultural systems but his rural, green lustiness reminds us that without this holy, primitive force we would soon become (like the dinosaurs) totally sterile and ultimately quite extinct.

GRAPES: A good sign of wealth and plenty, also a signal that a difficult project is soon about to come to fruition.

GRASS: Like sea, land and sky etc, any large expanse in dreams parallels the subconscious mind. Green healthy looking grass is analogous with clear logical-thinking. Alternatively, poor darkened matted grasses are connected with turmoil and anxieties.

GUITAR: Soft melodious playing arises from seductive and romantic desires whilst aggressive, loud music gives evidence of the more troubled, immature mind - time to give vent to pent up wishes and liberate yourself from the stifling rut which surrounds you.

GULL: Another bird that depicts greed and selfishness, also, because of its water association, a sign of sea voyage.

GUN: Primarily a dominant phallic symbol. Guns are very similar to expensive sports cars because they may display the need to project ego-force to be noticed. They are a status symbol for the owner (dreamer). Consider the proud peacock showing off his bright plumage and you will get the same inherent message, psychologically suggestive of inordinate sexual stimulation or even premature ejaculation. It's also a token of sudden disastrous occurrences which may test your abilities to the full. Beware of enemies posing as friends for skulduggery is at hand.

HAMMER: Much depends on the light in which the hammer is viewed. To break rocks with one means that you will win through problems after a hard struggle. To see one in the sky is a good herald of excellent opportunities coming soon. The hammer that sparks is a sign of creative and divine inspiration; your life will take on a new meaning.

HAND: A hand with fingers pointing at you tells you to think well about your proposed course of action. The gods, in their wisdom, are warning you to analyse a situation, which may seem satisfactory but is actually quite dangerous in some way. A raised open palm tells you to stop and think because plans may go astray. Hands are (like faces) physical expressions of emotional force. They act as great guides and sometimes guardians too. In the realm of dreams and vision don't ever ignore them.

HARE: Queen Boudicca released a hare from the folds of her cloak both as a rite for spiritual conciliation and for divination before engaging Roman forces in battle. The hare has been regarded as a sacred shape-shifting animal since very ancient times. On the subconscious level it denotes stamina with ability to avoid obstacles. It also signifies indecisiveness because of its tendency to quickly switch direction when evading predators. The ancients regarded hares as a lunar animal sacred to the Moon Goddess. The Chinese saw it as being essentially feminine connected with the Yin principal of creation. Because of this we may link it to the anima (feminine and Goddess aspect) when it is seen in a man's dream. We can observe a very old link to monotheistic female suppression here if we examine the Hebrew representation of this creature. To them it symbolised, because of its feminine aspect, lust and wanton fecundity. The Old Testament describes hares as being "unclean". This term was often used to denigrate menstruating women into second-class citizens. In old farming communities the last sheaf of corn to be cut in a field was believed to contain the corn spirit. This god was frequently depicted as an animal, often given the form of a hare. Could the term 'harvest' originate from an older more colloquial phrase hare-vest and hare-feast and hare-festival?

HARP: Love and romance are never far away from this sign. There is however a certain amount of pent-up stress and emotion inherent in the harp's laboured structural composition. The love aspect is evident in the swan-like structure of the harp. The swan is very closely linked with the Celtic god of love and beauty, Angus. His father the Dagda possessed a wooden harp which played all by itself and brought the seasons into order. Angus too had a harp but unlike his father's instrument it was made of gleaming gold. When Angus played it was impossible to resist the charm of his sweet melodies. The harp is an ancient part of our native cultural romance. Without doubt it is an excellent harbinger of love and longing passions aroused.

HAWK: Similar attributes as the falcon. Sometimes connects with feelings of cruelty to other people that stand in your way or work against you.

HELMET: A symbol that projects associations with the higher intellect or even spirituality. The helmet covers that part of you which is prized by many as the centre of being. An open helmet signifies trustworthiness, whilst a closed visor indicates sinister intentions against the viewer by some other unknown party.

HERBS: Herbs are really too wide a ranging subject to lump together under one generalisation, however for the sake of simplicity I shall state that they link subconsciously with the psyche. Any substance that possesses the ability to heal or kill impresses the human mind much more than we realise at face value. Herbs connect to myth, legend and most of all to magic. No Pagan rite would be complete without its correct portion of herbs, either for use in incense of otherwise. Each plant is connected to a different god-form or planetary virtue i.e. dill, fern and marjoram lie beneath the dominion of Mercury, whilst Venus claims the possession of golden rod, elder and the sorrels.

HILL: Green pleasant hillsides in summer tells us that any problems faced in life will soon be conquered. The inability to surmount difficult hills means that there is a strong chance of unwelcome attentions from other individuals soon.

HOOD: Secrets of the mind and beyond are indicated when the hood comes into vision. Like the helmet, this is a head covering but the hood occludes all facial features. It hides the true emotions and prevents the viewer from knowing what lies beneath. The hood can be a positive image e.g. the hooded (heroic) figure of Robin Hood. Alternatively, it may be negative, having associations with dread, fear and the realms of death, for instance, the hooded terror of the Inquisition's priestly-torturers or even the black, apocalyptic image of the hooded Grim Reaper. The hood encourages us to discover something that's unknown, something that we must eventually face, which is presently hidden from our common worldly perception. It then epitomises occult wisdom.

HORNS: Horns are an ancient sign of fecundity and sensuality. To see them in dreams is an omen of sexual prowess in a man and fruitfulness in a woman. The early church took all the ancient Pagan horned gods of nature (eg Pan and Cernunnos and Faunus etc.) and changed them into Satanic-forces. The Council of Toledo defined the Devil to have cloven hooves and a horned head in 447 CE. Society is still trying to pull itself out of the spiritual morass caused by this dangerous thought-form. Psychologists, healers and sex-counsellors are still dealing with the inherent ramifications of this cheerless doctrine against natural, life-creating passion and fertility. This man-made illusion has disrupted the psychic balance of life and the sooner it is abandoned by us the better it will be for our species as a whole.

HORSE: Horses are sacred to numerous deities. The waves of the sea are attributed to the Greek Poseidon and the Celtic Manannan and (or) the Roman Neptune. The god Mars had horse races held in his honour during the months of March and October. The sudden unexpected appearance of a horse was deemed to be an ill omen of death and destruction. Odin/ Woden rode an eight-legged Horse (Sleipnir) through the sky. This symbol is closely connected with man's animal nature and survival instincts. Seeing yourself in control of a wild horse is to master these lower, sometimes negative aspects of self that can threaten the higher intellectual capacity. A wild uncontrollable steed running joyfully is the ultimate symbol of freedom and liberation. How it relates to the individual is a matter for serious thought. At the risk of generalisation, the horse can be regarded as a beneficent, yet most dynamic of symbols.

HORSESHOE: Old sign of wonder and magic. Iron that fashions the horseshoe has magical associations. It was thought to ward off mischievous fairies and elves. The shape of the horseshoe is crescent-like so naturally it acquired a certain connection with lunar deities such as Diana, Hecate and Luna. Incidentally, Epona is the Romano and Celtic horse-goddess, so we should also remember this powerful deity's association with this old symbol. The horseshoe remains the perfect symbol of good luck and psychic protection.

HYENA: If you are down on your luck and life is giving back nothing but sadness and sorrow, then symbols like the hyena may be experienced. This can also be a warning sign that somebody or something is plotting against you. Time to watch your back and count your friends with care.

INK: To spill ink is a warning against libels either by the viewer or directed against him and her. To write with ink is a sign of creativity and increased mental awareness.

INQUISITION: To be brought before such an authority is a sign of deep worries, guilt complexes and emotional trauma. To belong to an inquisition underlies a negative streak bordering on the sadistic that if not quickly checked within the holder will eventually result in self-destructive or self-defeating tendencies. Fundamentalism always seeks to censor, silence or eventually slaughter its critics in the name of doing the common good or confronting evil. The dark side of human nature where evil poses as good never resides far under the surface of human insecurities. The inquisition sign warns in no uncertain terms to guard against becoming too pious in your opinions against other members of the human race. Be tolerant.

IRON: Iron is weight and weight is extra luggage that you can well do without. This is especially so in the sense thus it may depict worries. Iron is connected with protection. Our early ancestors must have felt a lot better with a strong iron lance at their side as opposed to the older, more breakable stone implement. Iron was power and the sign of prestige and defence. Iron is fashioned out of the elements of Mother Earth. Iron has the ability to earth or redirect energy and because of this it has always had a place in the realms of magical workings. It can be blessed mark of the Thunder God in all his multifarious guises, and is also closely connected with the fire god, Vulcan. An open-minded individual will quickly discover further links here between the Sacred-Hammer, passion and the emotions within.

IVY: Priests of the god of rebirth (Attis) wore ivy leaf tattoos upon their bodies. It was eaten during rites of Bacchus to inspire and adherents into greater intimacy with the god – to connect with the spirit-force of the deity. The ancients wore ivy crowns to prevent excess intoxication and poets particularly valued them. Osiris also held ivy as his sacred plant. It also has associations with Thalia (the Muse of comedy). The plant is a very hardy evergreen and quick to colonise old cottages thus it brings to mind survival against hard odds and qualities of resurrection. Ivy turns man-made ugliness into natural beauty. To see this plant in vision is a sign of longevity and endurance. It can also be a symbol of sadness, decay, melancholy and unrequited love.

JACKAL: The symbolism of this scavenger follows a similar form to that of the hyena. The Jackal frequently appears after we have experienced great sadness in life; time to "pick up the pieces" and move on to greener pastures.

JACKDAW: Beware of family arguments and disputes that may arise from seemingly small insignificant affairs. The jackdaw, because of its sociable nature, has links with the aspect of safety in numbers. The scavenging habits of this species suggests an association with frugality of emotion.

JAWS: Jaws of savage beasts in vision have always been a powerful symbol of danger and strength. Because jaws tear meat they also connect with feelings about revenge and sometimes even justice. Today, the sign of jaws also lends itself to associations with libel, slander and all types of malicious gossip. Loose mouths are always a danger to freethinkers.

JOURNEY: For a depressed person to dream of a fond journey denotes the desire for happiness. For the rich and affluent man to see a trip into dark foreboding places suggests underlying guilt and subconscious worries about failure in the world of business.

JUDGE: Impending justice and final judgement concerning a pressing issue. The judge stands for ultimate authority. Your past actions are soon to be used against you in either a positive or negative manner. The judge is the hand of karmic justice working towards you. Every action has its final price.

KALEIDOSCOPE: Abstract events with little concrete foundation. Your imagination may be getting carried away with itself.

KANGAROO: A sign of transformation. The young joey snuggles warmly inside mum's pouch. The adults suddenly spring off at great speed without warning, changing direction with gazelle-like ease. The animal can also lash out its hind legs with immense power to inflict harm on pursuers. To see the kangaroo in dreams and visions is a sign that one will achieve success by outwitting jealous rivals or foes.

KESTREL: This little bird of prey can be viewed in a similar fashion as other falcon and hawk type of hunters. Because of modern mans' intrusion into the countryside with new road schemes, this bird has quickly learnt the art of the scavenger and will add carrion to its diet if the opportunity arises. Thanks to man, the kestrel's role in symbolism is becoming one that contains darker aspects of transformation.

KEY: The symbol of Janus, god of doorways and new beginnings. A key unlocks a door and the door in this instance may relate to forthcoming events either good or bad. See the key as a herald of change and exciting new opportunities to come. Freedom and liberation from an oppressive situation are also strongly indicated by this powerful symbol. The Egyptian cross (Ankh) is the hieroglyph for the key to life and living. Its key-like structure represents an initiation into spiritual grace and wisdom. It may show us that we stand at an important crossroads in the life-quest.

KILLING: To kill is a sign of repressed, negative feelings against someone or something in your life. To be killed in a dream marks a desire to escape a disconcerting situation that seems temporarily out of your control. Death is not a final thing but a mere change of direction, a way to leave the past in order to start a new life. A worrying future operation, driving test or job interview can trigger a series of nightmares associated with this dark topic.

KINGFISHER: A blessing from the gods that lifts the spirit high. It heralds good news and gifts from unexpected quarters.

KITE: Flying a kite is a sign of freedom and hope. It is also connected with the realms of childhood and days of liberation and innocence. If the kite breaks away into the sky expect a swift resolution to an important problem soon. It forms a special connection between air and earth.

KNOTS: In magical workings knots are storage receptacles for concentrated energy. They lock in force that would otherwise escape. They are traps then for whatever we wish to put into them. On dream levels they may depict problems that cannot seem to be mastered. With wisdom there will be a sure solution. It's just a matter of interpreting it and untying the knot. Try hard, be sincere in your manner and the gods will always show you the right direction to take.

LADDER: Advancement or retreat is the message given by this sign. Think of the simple game children play, Snakes and Ladders. To put it simply, see this sign as a statement of your life and how well or badly it's progressing. It's often a warning of a fall in social standing, high time to assess your current situation. To walk under a ladder is considered bad luck in popular superstition. This may be because a leaning ladder forms a triangle that is the old, elemental sign of fire. Walking into such a sign can then be said to invite the destructive quality of this element into your life. With the correct knowledge and preparation all elemental work is safe and beneficial, however fire element must never be treated lightly.

LAKE: A lake is a special place of hidden mystery. Even when dead calm, a beautiful lake exudes a sense of brooding power and majesty. It links intimately with our emotions. The sick and low of spirit will also benefit greatly from being close to gentle waters of a lake. In dreams the action of the lake (either calm or turbulent) represents the highs and lows of the emotions and their resultant, concomitant impression on your life. On a baser level a mother of toddlers may see this as a symbol of profuse urination.

LAMB: To parents, the lamb is linked to their children. "My little lamb." and similar sentiments illustrate this point quite clearly. The lamb is the sign of innocence, so any vision, which involves cruelty to them denotes harm coming to the observer or their own offspring. Much of the lamb's earlier connection with sacrifice can be traced to the grossly sickening laws on burnt offerings, found in the book of Leviticus in the Bible. It is strange that even today such an innocent creature should still be treated so badly. The vile horrors of intensive factory farming will unfortunately ensure that the lamb continues to suffer needlessly for the desires of mankind.

LAMP: To see a lamp in the darkness is a sign of hope. It is also a symbol of spiritual awakening deep within the viewer. In the Tarot the image of the Hermit carrying his lamp shows us that the lonely path can lead to illumination. Away from the crowd and the common herd-instincts of man there is the promise of mystical grace and wisdom. The lamp then may be seen as an offer of a spiritual quest from the Old Gods themselves.

LARK: If ever there was a creature to exhibit the soaring, lofty heights of spiritual grace then the skylark must surely be top of the list. This pretty little bird possesses, with its beautiful song and rapid ascending flight, the ability to aspire poets to great works. To dream of the lark is to feel nature's creative energy that resides deep within us all. It's the bird that links us to our spiritual essence and beyond. To the sad and disheartened it represents hope, to lovers it denotes fidelity and joy. Celebrate its vision.

LAWYER: Possible guilt complexes rising to the surface of your consciousness, something long forgotten from the past coming back to haunt the viewer. This is a symbol of legal authority and the deep mind's way of gaining attention over a pressing matter. The prudent are wise to investigate this sign and put matters to right. It's also a warning of criticism, especially in the work place.

LEOPARD: The Leopard cannot change his spots and as such this animal is a sign that danger lurks in the most unlikely of situations. The unseen and unheard stalker in usually the one that gets you so to see the leopard on higher levels is a sure warning from the Old-Ones to beware of menace posing as serene beauty. The savage spirit-cat draws its life-breath from our deepest fears.

LETTERS: Generally speaking letters depict communication.. Good letters containing fine news herald just that. Letters that cause upset denote mishaps and possible loses in terms of friendships, money and business or love. Anonymous letters warn of deceitfulness and skulduggery by an unknown assailant. Letters from old friends tell that they are thinking about you and will soon make contact either by mail or otherwise. Today, 'email' may have taken on similar aspects in dreamtime imagery.

LIGHTENING: This is the physical manifestation of divine light that can destroy and also create life. The druidic priests of the Celts held sacred any oak that was touched by the gods with lightening. The god of lightening was Taranis (or possibly Sucellos). To the Romans he was Jupiter-Fulgar, whilst the Etruscans knew him simply as Tin. To see lightening in dreams heralds important changes in your life. It also depicts an initiation from one state of being to another. When the divine light of the Old Gods shines upon your soul, see it as a blessing of good things to come after hardships have been conquered.

LINNET: Another attractive little bird, the cock linnet's rosy breast is emblematic of summer days and childish enthusiasm, a beneficent sign of happy events to come.

LION: Lions are symbolic of achieving great goals; moreover they are sacred to many solar gods and goddesses. They signify awesome power in nature and man. Because of their all consuming and devouring aspect they also represent the eternal qualities of time itself. The lion stands as probably the most potent vision of triumph and valour known to mankind. This aspect of victory is certainly not only to be perceived in a militaristic sense. The Egyptian goddess Tefnut was often depicted as a lioness; she was the presiding deity of moisture. Without water there is no life so in this context we see the lion gaining victory over the realm of drought and ultimately death itself.

LIZARD: A symbol of minor irritations. The lizard is a smaller version of the snake and this in turn leads us to that mythical totem of life force, the dragon. Because of their quick actions they also denote unexpected accidents and misadventures.

LLAMA: Somewhat like a cross between a horse and a camel, with the camel part gaining in prominence. Its slow beast of burden characteristics give this animal symbolic ties with creatures like the mule and the ass. View the llama as a steady sign of durability in life's adverse conditions.

LOBSTER: Anything with sharp claws that crawls out of the water should be viewed with caution. Water, especially deep-sea water is linked to the subconscious mind. The lobster, because of its rich food association, can be a beneficent sign.

Also, because of the way that lobsters change colour after being boiled, they are symbolic of transformation. A lot depends on how close your life revolves around such a symbol. A trawlerman's vision of a lobster will be vastly different from an office worker's view of the same thing.

LOVE: Contentment, affection, happiness, friendships and beautiful romances are all foretold with this vision. Your life is (or soon shall be) satisfying and wholesome. Venus will enter your life and make everything seen perfect if you open your heart to her blessings. Don't become too complaisant - although love is absolutely essential to a full life it is but only one aspect. Balance in all things is the key to true happiness. Without love on all levels of existence perversion can easily set in. This is particularly true on the physical plane when the lack of bodily attention and affection leads to sexual obsession. In the name of the Goddess, it is our duty as citizens of Planet-Earth to spread love wherever and whenever we can.

MAGNET: A path of attraction is calling you from your normal interests. This may relate to the physical attraction of an admirer or an offer of wealth and success from a business associate. Care is needed as the alluring pull of these charms may have hidden qualities. When a body is drawn into the orbit of another the former may eventually find it impossible to escape.

MAGPIE: "One for sorrow two for joy, three for a girl and four for a boy, five for silver, six for gold, seven for a secret never to be told." The crafty old magpie is steeped in native folklore. Its striking black and white plumage is reminiscent of other creatures that connect with aspects of duality. The magpie's harsh raucous chatter is symbolic of malicious gossip. Moreover, its shrewd eating habits are closely linked to human theft.

MARCH: To be included in a military march against your will is a sign of oppression and the desire for self-liberation. To partake in one as a volunteer marks the wish for power and the attention of others. The march is, in effect, the viewer's will forcing itself upon what it sees as lesser mortals.

MASK: To wear a mask is to conceal an aspect of yourself. Subconsciously, the mask symbolises mystery, deceit, danger and licentious affairs. This concealment may come from fear - the mask stops your true nature being examined by others. Contemporary masked heroic comic-strip figures like Batman and Spiderman have ensured that the mask is also a symbol of unexpected assistance when most needed. Mankind will always love a dashing masked hero or villain because they represent a braver side of us that usually remains suppressed and untested deep within the subconscious mind.

MEDAL: The wish for glory, fame and greater recognition from friends and colleagues, the desire to be noticed and taken into consideration. Old tatty medals are a sign of disappointment and sadness or even long lost relatives from days gone by.

MICE: The sign that domestic and family affairs are getting too much for you, time to take a break away from the humdrum everyday aspects of life.

MINEFIELD: Obstacles in life that pose an immediate threat. These obstacles may not but be recognised but they could be endangering you from any direction. Beware of gossip and slanderous accusations both from others and by yourself.

MIRROR: A symbol sacred of the Moon-Goddess and the reflective element of water. Magical mirrors have been used through the ages in similar fashion to the crystal ball. Thus mirrors link with divination and the magical arts. Any reflective image has the ability to quieten the chattering mind and allow a deeper connection with the hidden world. In dreams and vision, mirrors symbolise analytical periods in life when we need to stand back and take a long hard look at events. Mirrors are also doorways to greater spiritual awareness.

MOLE: Because of the way moles burrow about unseen by human eyes, they are analogous with hidden worries. Anything that blindly tunnels along like the mole is symbolic of arguments and strife as to go ahead without direction is to invite certain trouble and misfortune.

MONGOOSE: This animal is well known for its snake-killing abilities. The snake is symbolic of earth-energy so we may perceive the mongoose as its master. It ranks as a powerful emblem of overcoming great, seemingly impossible adversities.

MONKEY: Many species of monkey are tainted with the image of "snatch, grab and run." In nature this is a natural survival instinct, but in modern human society it is wholly taboo. The monkey then, in dreams, is the thief and rascal. To see him is a warning to "keep your hand on your ha'penny."

MOON: Dreams of the moon belong to the spiritual realm. They also mark the feminine side of divinity i.e. the Lunar Goddess. In a man's dream the moon represents the feminine aspect of his nature and the intuitive, nourishing and formative part of himself that often lies suppressed. To a woman the moon stands for her fulfilment in life and the fertilising aspect within. The moon links with the menstrual-cycle lasting one month and the waxing, full and waning aspects of the moon correspond with the feminine fertility period. Whilst the sun symbolises the harsh, visual light of day and the conscious mind, the moon is very much the reverse i.e. the unknown face of night, magic and the subconscious mind.

MOORHEN: Emblematic of quarrels and family disputes. Their aggressive behaviour towards intruders is symbolic of human territoriality and the will to repel invaders. To see them in a vision is a warning to defend your position against enemies.

MOUNTAIN: Pleasant climbs up gentle inclines denote success in any future enterprise. Hard, dangerous climbs up wet, slippery mountains foretell of failure and accidents ahead. Take time to examine your situation and you might be able to save yourself a great deal of disappointment. The mountain is a challenge in one form or another. Spiritually, it depicts the heavens and sky (God) conjoining with the earth (Goddess) to bring forth life and fruitful abundance.

MUSEUM: A symbol of childhood and nostalgia. If the images in the scene are good then your background is quite sound but if you are disturbed by the exhibits then some part of your past has resurfaced to plague you. The answer to your problem will be there somewhere, you just have to analyse the messages that the gods are sending you through the vehicle of your subconscious mind.

NAVY: War ships on a steady course are emblematic of victory over strong adversaries and problems. They also stand for regaining health after illness. To see a navy sink is a sign of overdoing things and mental strain.

NET: Entrapment, captivation and evangelization on various levels. To net something or be netted means that one has set a plan in motion or is frustrated by disappointments or delays respectively. The net links with death and the watery (subconscious) realm for obvious reasons. Gladiators armed with sword and shield once faced the grave danger of the Retiarius (fighter armed with trident and net). The depths of the sea remind us of the net used to haul in Neptune's harvest. The net is also (like a spider's web) the instrument which seizes the unwary traveller and denies them access to their true path. I would suggest that one should view this symbol with much respect, for it may be a timely warning from the gods that all is not well in your life at present.

NIGHTJAR: This bird's nocturnal, reclusive nature gives it a close link to the sinister. It denotes all that remains unknown or unseen. We must remember that sometimes we need to unleash ourselves in order to discover deeper, hidden levels of self that dwell within. The unknown should not always be feared for numerous inventions have been revealed through the brave experiments of many mystical pioneers. To fear these levels is to fear aspects of yourself. The nightjar would make an excellent totem for all brave psychonauts into the unknown, those hardy souls who would liberate their self from the mundane in order to seek out the sacred mystical places residing within.

NUNS: Because of the aspect of alienation from normal society, dreams and visions of nuns foretell of subconscious feelings of solitude, widow-hood, grief, taboo, desires and illicit love affairs. Also denotes indoctrinated sexual guilt and repulsion of natural human desires.

NURSE: If a nurse is visiting you in vision then take care of your health for this is a strong sign that all is not well. The nurse is also a desire for attention and relief from the humdrum problems of daily life. She, or he, stands as a mediator between you and the doctor thus the nurse is a barrier between your and the fear of the surgeon's knife. In this context the nurse becomes a defender protecting you from the terrors of the unknown. See the nurse then as a guardian, albeit one who reminds us of those dark things residing deep within ourselves which we would often rather not face.

NUTHATCH: This small bird's habit of creeping up trees in search of insects is symbolically similar to our incessant quest for knowledge. See it as a sign of progress and personal evolution.

NYMPHS: A nymph is a wild aspect of divinity, a nature spirit inhabiting streams and woodlands. To see one in dream and vision is a sign of passion, love and sexuality. The love may not be for another human but for nature and life itself.

OCTOPUS: This creature of the deep has eight tentacles, because of this it has associations with the spider. Aspects of entrapment are then quite obvious. The figure eight is symbolic of balance (two circles joined). The octopus and squid gave numerous nightmares to sailors of old. Something that rises up out of dark waters (the subconscious) has to be seen as a threat. This is especially so if the thing in question possesses eight large tentacles to grab you with. See it then as a warning of dangerous events to come.

OIL: Black crude is a sign of wealth and also reminds us of pollution and catastrophe in nature. Oil, in the sense of oils for beauty and health, are signs of contact. In magic, oil transports the essence of the aura to a given object or person. In aromatherapy, oil draws on the essences of plants (which have in turn condensed sun-energy in their own special way) to grant one health-giving favours. Oil in cookery is a sign of worldly desire and the need for attention. Oil is accordingly a sign of transportation of one element or level into another. The type of oil seen is the type of blessing or threat to be expected, albeit in symbolic fashion. An open mind and the need for discernment are the keys to understanding such images in dream and vision.

ONIONS: These have an old reputation for being good to combat colds and chill. Magically they are used for banishing negativity and to promote courage as they come under the influence of Mars. To dream of onions is to realise that there is a threat to your well-being close at hand. Identify it and you will be victorious.

ORANGES: Sacred to the Sun God. Oranges are a good sign of riches and plenty. Used magically to boost the aura and purify, they are an excellent image to aid in visualisation, generally a symbol of satisfaction, wealth and success.

OTTER: Otters represent dexterity and wisdom. The manner in which they lie on their backs to crack open shellfish is analogous with man surmounting problems. Their habit of dipping then rising in tranquil streams is symbolic of the human quest for knowledge. An altogether satisfactory totem of satisfactory events to come.

OUZEL: The ouzel denotes the search for hidden knowledge. This bird is a creature of watery places like rivers. Because of this link with water it more properly connects with feminine, intuitive, nourishing, goddess aspects rather than the fertilising, masculine god face of self. For a man to see it in dreams is a sign of the anima, the feminine and sensitive essence residing within his being. For a woman it denotes the many aspects making up her feminine, instinctive self.

OWL: What the eagle is to the Sun and Sky God, the Owl is to the Lunar Goddess. This bird of night stands for wisdom that is hidden and unknown. The Egyptians associated the owl with death and passivity. It is the power of mystery, magic and imagination. It is easy to connect this bird to negativity but out of life comes death, out of death we see new life. The owl's association with moon goddesses like Hecate also connects with old-crone and wise-one aspects and divination. Do not fear the owl but instead listen to its inner wisdom with a still, receptive mind.

OX: Similar associations with other horned animals like the bull, goat and the ram, an agricultural sign of continuity and evolutionary progress on any level.

OYSTERCATCHER: Bird of the wide-open spaces on lonely shorelines, symbolic of life, liberation and freedom from repressive influences. Its black and white coloration is linked to dualistic concepts in creation.

PALACE: To see yourself in a plush palace full of riches is a sign of increasing fortune. A ramshackle palace that is in a state of decay is symbolic of lost opportunities and sad events troubling the viewer.

PANCAKE: An economical or even overtly parsimonious situation is set to affect the viewer if pancakes are seen. Tossing pancakes is however analogous with the chance for liberation from life-worries and stress.

PANTHER: Sign of unseen forces working against the observer - unexpected events occurring out of the blue. Imminent danger.

PANTOMIME: The surrealism embracing this comic vision tells the viewer that life is not always as it seems. Mistrust and deceit are waiting around the corner for the unwary. The strange characters in the pantomime are often shadows of real individuals whom we know well. Their actions in the scene foretell of their intentions towards us, which sometimes we would rather not know about.

PARTRIDGE: This bird's alarming habit of waiting until one is virtually upon it before shooting off from cover gives rise to links with unexpected surprises. It denotes shock, moodiness and unexpected confrontations that crop up without warning. It can also be linked to aspects of chicken-like silliness because of its odd nature.

PATH: Much depends on the sort of path encountered. A lonely crossroads foretells of important decisions ahead. A quiet, straight pathway tells us that life is presently set to be calm and uneventful. A twisting path is a sign of pleasure and fun times ahead. A steep uphill path warns of hardship and troubles to come.

PEA: Symbolic of good fortune, wealthy dealings and help from others. Their colour links with the good earth and this marks the worldly bounty that they promise. Especially a good sign for farmers, gardeners and anyone else connected with horticulture.

PEEWIT: Also known as the lapwing or green plover. This bird is seen in huge flocks as winter closes in. It is tied to feelings of continuity and social interaction. See it as a fine symbol of friendship and glad-tidings to come.

PELICAN: Intimately connected with the sea and thus the subconscious mind. Their symbolism may be seen as being very much like that of the gannet.

PENCIL: To write with a pencil marks the desire to communicate with others, even so much as to be a serious demand for attention. To see others writing with pencils displays a subconscious wish to find out a secret. It can also represent a need to be noticed and treated with affection.

PERFUME: Pleasant aromas in dream and vision are not uncommon. Perfume is a sign of romance, sexuality and unadulterated lust. There is a certain note of whirlwind affairs and glamour involved here too, which may warn of the break-up of present stable relationships.

PHEASANT: Very strong connection here with luxury and opulence because of its beautiful coloured plumage. The pheasant, like the partridge, also shoots out from cover in an alarming fashion, so it may be tied to sudden shock etc. It is a powerful warning to be thrifty with financial and business dealings.

PIER: This image stretches deep into the sea and because water is often analogous with the subconscious: the pier becomes a trip into the unknown regions of the mind and beyond. To stand firmly upon a solid pier is symbolic of strong mental ability and the desire to be victorious. To see a pier sink into the sea is a warning that one must change course in life soon or else trouble will occur.

PIG: An animal of the good earth. The old maxim "happy as pigs in muck" gives us a clue to the role, which this beast plays in symbolic interpretation. The mere thought of pigs happily grovelling about in mud has a comical air to it. The author is actually chuckling right now with this vision in mind. Pigs then are a beneficent, slightly jovial if not overindulgent sign of pleasant events to come.

PIGEON: Symbolic of travel and the ability to communicate with others. Often heralds news that has been long in coming, possibly in the form of an important letter through the post.

PIPE: A length of pipe (as used in industry) is without doubt a symbol that contains phallic connotations. However, the smoking pipe is associated with wisdom, (the peace pipe) advice and contentment. It also depicts a transportation of the water element, ergo the thought process and its delivery.

PIRATE: Often given as a sign of deceit, theft and false hopes. This may be so in the majority of cases however the pirate can also be emblematic of freedom, bravado and liberation from oppressive forces. The pirate's link to the sea (subconscious) suggests connections to a disturbed mind, which requires addressing rather quickly.

POISON: To be poisoned in dreams denotes others working surreptitiously against your best interests. To be the poisoner marks a desire to eradicate problems that seem to be overwhelming you. Also a sign of revenge against what you regard as personal injustice.

POPE: Symbol of religious servitude and authority, also, because of infamous historical misdemeanours, a mark of cruelty and injustice against minorities. This latter remark is today further strengthened when we consider the latest Vatican statement against Paganism that seeks to place the blame for the Nazi Holocaust on the heads of Pagans.

PORCUPINE: Although not an altogether negative symbol, the porcupine is a sign of reluctance. Nobody in their right mind wants to get too close to those nasty sharp quills - also a symbol of self-defence and defiance against greater odds.

POSTMAN: A sign of unexpected news arriving. Also, anxiety and indecision are possible connections here.

PRAIRIE DOG: Their fast responsive actions say it all. This animal is a sign of the alert mind and everything that links with the mundane consciousness. To see it in dreamtime is a warning to beware of unexpected assaults from hidden foes.

PRIEST: This sign marks all guilt, oppression, authority, hardship, misery and serfdom. Priesthoods (of any category) have always been instigated to stop the populace from gaining direct links to divinity. They act as a type of spiritual middleman between the adherent and his chosen god. Can you see through the confusion of the middleman image?

PYRAMID: This ancient image has associations with heat and fire, not only the fire of hot situations like Egypt where these vast structures are found but the fire of the human spirit. See them as a sign in visions of enlightenment and wisdom for their Pagan heritage holds many secrets as but still undiscovered by modern man.

QUAIL: Sign of minor successes and fair dealings with business associates, symbolic of inheritance and gifts from afar, altogether a very favourable omen.

QUICKSAND: A negative symbol of misfortune and events that the conscious mind wishes to hush-up. It also marks the desire to escape responsibilities.

RACCOON: Very much (like the monkey) a sign of theft. Also symbolic of betrayal - if you see this you should examine your relationships with others. Things may not be quite as rosy as they at first appear.

RAFT: To sail away in a raft from a place of captivity denotes the wish for liberation. To sail a raft into stormy waters foretells of unhappy events ahead, especially in personal relationships.

RAILWAY: A sign of communication and travel to far places. These places may however not be of the physical world, they frequently represent ambitions which you are set to achieve in life. The state of the track and vehicles indicate this image's positive or negative meaning.

RAINBOW: Symbolic of happy events and great success. The gold at the end of the rainbow doubtless refers to spiritual enlightenment. Expect to gain greater awareness after seeing this lovely sign.

RAKE: Hard work and endurance are suggested here. A broken rake is a warning of misfortune in the work place.

RAT: The Rat denotes illness, injury and deception. It stands as a warning that life's little problems are becoming too much to deal with. Like the mouse, this sign urges us to take a break and leave the 'rat-race' behind.

RAVEN: This bird is a sign of death and ill omen; however it is not all negative. The Celts regarded it as a creature of divination. It was two ravens that warned the hero god Lugh of the advancing forces of his enemies, the Fomarian giants. The Norse God Odin had two ravens, Hunin and Munin (Thought and Memory) that he sent out each morning to gather news of worldly events. Christians demonised the poor old raven into a sign of the Devil. In Pagan philosophy life and death go hand in hand, as do aspects of divination and death. Death and divination are not evil they are essential rooms in the house of life. The raven exhibits this truth well. He comes to us as a vital warning not an evil enemy.

REINDEER: Symbolic of winter's months and Yuletide. It can also be seen as a sign of hardship being conquered by perseverance. Stick to your plans and don't let others dissuade you from your goals.

RHUBARB: View it as a symbol of fast growth in business and relationships tempered with possible mishaps caused by lack of attention to detail.

RINGS: Rings are complete circle. Because rings are frequently made from precious stones and gold, they stand for wealth and prosperity. They denote love, friendships and lasting memories, albeit sometimes marked by nostalgic sadness. Their condition (dull or shiny) gives us a clue as to their relevant meaning.

RIVER: Rivers are, in a fashion, the veins of Mother Earth. They denote the transposition of energy from one place to another. They remind us that life is never static but always moving; they represent emotions that change on a constant basis from good to bad and vice versa. Rivers link with therapeutic values for there is no finer a place to be than the healing water's edge when illness threatens.

ROBIN: A sign of the approaching winter, also symbolic of the life-in-death aspect in the natural cycle. Its red breast is emblematic of hope in times of trouble, the bright spark of life that always returns anew.

ROOF: "Shout it from the roof-tops." This old maxim is linked to celebration and bliss. Being on a roof is to gain advancement and prestige. However, to fly from a high roof may denote astral travel (actual or wished for). Falling from one is a warning of possible impending disaster. Realise and come to terms your fears instead of suppressing them.

ROOK: A symbol of death because of its coloration and crow-like nature. The rook also stands for family squabbles and disputes.

SAND: On one hand it marks the fear on loss and poverty, but it may also represent the desire for holidays, fun and love. If accompanied by feelings of thirst, wake up and take a drink and eat less salt with your food.

SCEPTRE: A regal sign of good fortune and prosperity. Expect to achieve your ambitions soon. Also a symbol of being in charge of a situation that other people fear.

SCORPION: This sign has sexual connotations. The sting in the tail aspect is generally considered to be phallic and emblematic of the act of male ejaculation.

SCYTHE: The instrument of the Grim Reaper and a symbol of death, change and removal. This need not be an image to fear because the death aspect may be more connected with death of a situation. The scythe of the Reaper must remove the old in order to bring in the new. This is the prime law of the universe and we must realise its inherent wisdom. See it primarily as a forewarning to modify your ways and improve your present situation.

SEAL: A creature that dwells in two elements, the water and the earth. Because of its ungainly land movements but graceful swimming, this animal is symbolic of endeavouring to better your position in life.

SHRIKE: The butcherbird, as it is often called, is emblematic of wanton cruelty and violence. Its habit of impaling victims on thorns and barbed wire leaves little to question its meaning. To see it in divination is not a favourable omen. We could see in this bird associated with personal sacrifice in order to achieve our aims.

SKELETON: Taking away the vital life materials from a body and leaving it exposed as nothing more than white bones betokens injustice, offence and ailments directed toward the viewer, a significant caution to take good care. It also warns that unwanted events from the past may possibly require dealing with before the future can be secured.

SMOKE: We cannot see through thick smoke thus it holds secrets and intrigue. It is the hidden world just beyond the physical that contains fear, but at the same time fascination. Smoke also connects to fire element and human emotion. See it as a possible warning of deceit in romantic areas of your life. What lies behind the smoke may not be good for you. Also may denote news from afar, as in the Native American Indian smoke signal system.

SNAKE: One of the most ancient symbols of the serpent is to be seen on the Caduceus, two serpents twined round a winged staff and wand, the dual male and female creative forces of the cosmos. Snakes represent both equilibrium and good health. The snake can kill; it must in order to survive, but for modern man is a sign of death and ill omen once it stood as a symbol of earth-energy. When the serpent bites its own tail we see the completed circle of life and death and new life once again.

SOLDIER: Marching soldiers are a sign of order and established thinking. To be attacked by soldiers is a warning not to run before you can walk, or in other words, don't take on too many commitments which may cramp your style and weigh you down. Soldiers that are wounded are a sign of misfortune and unfulfilled ambitions.

SQUIRREL: Sign of the summer and good things therein. Squirrels are associated with trees and all things appertaining to them. They represent determined productivity and endurance.

STAG: The Stag, with its magical connection to the great horned God Cernunnos, needs no introduction. "This fabulous creature leads Pwyll into the underworld and represents the power of magical transformation." I first wrote these words in my previous work - *The Torch and the Spear*. Its antlers reach up high toward the heavens. They remind us of the twisted branches of trees; because of this the stag is connected to the growing energies inherent in the natural cycle. The stag is the magical escort that transports us between the levels and heralds change in both the spiritual and material realms.

STAIRS: To travel or even fall down stairs is symbolic of disappointment, fears and unhappy events. To go up stairways is evidence of social improvement and successful outcomes to pressing problems. Stairs are representative of travelling from one level of existence to another.

STARLING: The starling is the perfect exemplar of greediness. These gluttons devour every morsel on the bird table before smaller birds can even make an appearance. They stand for everything that is selfish and thoughtless toward others. If they have a saving grace it must be connected with the majestic beauty exhibited by their massive swirling flocks in winter. This spectacular sight is synchronised energy at its raucous best, energy that exemplifies the vital ebbing and flowing cycles of life.

STEEPLE: This image is closely linked to feelings of apprehension and misfortune. Like the Tower in the Tarot deck, it can frequently be an omen of destructive tendencies. This in itself may not be as bad as would first seem to be the case; the destruction of one establishment makes way for the new and (often) better one to come. It must be said that the phallic-shaped steeple also represents masculine fecundity and associated mating.

SUN: The sign of greatest wealth and abundance, especially if viewed at its midday zenith. The rising red sun is a promise of future hopes that will be fulfilled. The dying sun that slowly sets represents romantic nostalgia. The sun is the logical, clear mind as opposed to the instinctive and intuitive lunar realm. Without the life giving sun we are nothing. See it as a concomitant part of our ancient connection to nature and what lies beyond the mysteries of life, death and resurrection.

SWAN: In Celtic myth, Caer Ibormeith (the Dream-Maiden) and her companions turn into swans at the end of each summer. Angus, the god of love, changed himself into a swan and flew away with Caer to live happily ever after. Many other deities have shapeshifted into these beautiful birds. The swan is an ancient native symbol of transformation, grace and refined romance. White Swans are emblematic of prosperity and true love, whilst black swans warn us of forbidden romances that may lead to disaster.

SWORD: If shining and proper, a noble emblem of honour, courage and trust but if broken and rusty, a symbol of deceit, treachery and cowardice.

TABLE: Usually connects with feelings of good times with family and friends, the focal point of domestic life and decisions taken there. The (good or bad) state of the table indicates the current situation at home or what is soon to manifest. May also denote the school class-room and hidden emotions from your past.

TATTOO: This sign marks the desire to be special or to be noticed (loved) by others; hence it can be symbolic of insecurity and anxiety in social and romantic circles. Also connects with the exotic and strange, anything which diverges from the norm or institutionally-acceptable – an expressed desire to rebel against others.

TEETH: This symbol forms an important link to all that is essential for survival on planet earth. Teeth allow us to eat, fight and communicate feelings with other beings. Because of this they are signs of self-expression and the ego. To see teeth that fall out denotes illness and sorrow. To see white, sparkling teeth is symbolic of romance and happiness. Teeth that rip and tear are a warning of enemies that wish to destroy your reputation with slander and malice.

TERN: The old colloquial name for the tern was 'Sea swallow' because of its swooping flight pattern and forked tail. This bird attacks its prey in a similar fashion to larger sea birds, diving from height to kill small food fish. It is a symbol of dynamic energy, enjoyment and happy times to come.

THORN: Under nature's beauty lies a darker, more painful reality. The lovely rose, the sweet-scented hawthorn, the ubiquitous bramble remind the prudent to be aware that joy has to mingle with pain on all levels of existence. In layman's terms, see this vision as a sharp warning not to trust everything that appears, at first glance, to be trustworthy or alluring.

THRUSH: This bird is symbolic of hope and good fortune. The beautiful, euphoric melody of the song thrush needs no introduction. Its pure voice is enough to gladden the most disconsolate of hearts. It symbolises a magical feeling of spiritual renewal. However, there is another side to the thrush. Its habit of cracking open snails on hard rocks stands as a sign of endurance and the ability to master life's smaller problems.

TIGER: Symbolic of power, energy, superiority and sometimes cruelty. In eastern cultures it was linked to the new moon and the darker aspects of the human soul. Its lunar connection may be seen as the reverse of the lion's solar position. The beautiful striped skin of this beast denotes luxury and pleasure. The alternating dark and light pattern is suggestive of the principles of duality and equilibrium.

TOAD: Again like the frog, this little creature is (because of its metamorphosis from tadpole) linked to the aspect of transformation. The connection is however traditionally given as a more negative one than that of the frog simply because of the toad's dry, warty appearance. Its darker seemingly sinister countenance and persistently unnerving stare gave rise to a mediaeval association with evil and the Devil. All these negative connections did the toad no favours at all. They are in fact charming, quite fascinating animals with an ability to magnetise humans for considerable lengths of time. Their sinister aspect links them to the night, water and most especially the moon. They are emblematic of magic and the capacity to change direction at will.

TORTOISE: To see this animal's reflected image in waters or its appearance in rites of divination (such as the glowing embers of a fireplace) is a sign to slow down. It may also be viewed as a symbol of stagnation and lethargy. The gods will always show us what we need to know if we simply give them the space in our hearts to do so. The tortoise tells us that life is going at slow speed or alternatively that maybe it would be beneficial to take time out to have a well earned rest.

TURNSTONE: This little chap is often seen in massive flocks at the seaside where it hunts quickly for marine creatures before the tide turns. Symbolically speaking, the turnstone represents anxiety mixed with optimism. It's a sign that one is trying too hard to reach goals that may be achieved in easier fashion. This bird may also frequent your visions when you have lost something precious in life.

UNDERGROUND: Subterranean adventures or journeys are frequently astral tours into our own individual past histories. The underground realm is within us and can relate to deeply hidden emotions and fears. This is the dwelling place of the unknown. Since time immemorial, the mystics of old travelled to underground caverns to seek out the ancient truths which cannot be recorded in mere logical terms. These truths reside within each of us and must be experienced on a personal, intuitive level in order to be fully understood. This is one of the prime ambitions of magical practice for any genuine witch or shaman. To make known what was before wholly unknown and thus become a greater being.

URN: A link with the past and what has gone before, often associated with feelings of funerals and death. It can also relate to work and all that connects to it. It may represent a secret that must be discovered before personal evolution can progress.

VEIL: Symbolic of the unknown and fears attached to it. To see another person standing before you in a veil means that a stranger approaches who cannot be trusted. To view yourself veiled denotes a keen desire for intimacy and private situations, also a sign of change and initiation from one level of existence to another. A common example may be the veiled bride who leaves the wedding altar to start a very different life.

VOLCANO: The primordial forces of nature remind us that all of man's ambitions stand no chance against the awesome power of the gods. The volcano is destructive energy but at the same time it is sexual prowess that creates vital new life, an omen of big changes to come.

VULTURE: This gawky scavenger is probably Africa's equivalent to our own carrion eating birds such as the crow. The vulture is the bird of death and destruction. To see it in vision is not usually a welcome sight, although we must remember that death is an essential component in the cycle of life. Symbolically, vultures link with the Goddess in her darker, warlike, destroying, old-hag aspect. On the masculine side, vultures were once given as offerings to the Roman god of war, Mars. Many pre-Christian peoples viewed this creature as a sign of reincarnation and vital, spiritual transformation because of its (essential) corpse-eating habits. Romulus and Remus founded Rome after seeing portents involving vultures. They believed that the presence of these birds would ensure the creation of a powerfully warlike nation. The vulture is a gift from the gods, telling us to face hidden truths that we would prefer to ignore. The easiest way in life is not always the most beneficial path to follow. This bird can in spirit lead us into greater understanding of negative energies that must be challenged in order to achieve balance and harmony.

WAGTAIL: A bird of beautiful places, especially the yellow wagtail and its relative the grey wagtail. Its habit of darting out from a rock to snatch a passing river-fly is symbolic of our quest for universal knowledge. The river represents life drifting by, whilst we (as the wagtail) cast ourselves into the flow to grab what wisdom (the flies) we can along the way. The wagtail's frantic tail bobbing is also linked to ideas of impatience. This bird tells us to enjoy life by not allowing stress to become a problem.

WAITER: To be waited on denotes several possibilities - it may be the desire for luxuries. It may be linked to the need for personal power. It can be a sign of insecurity and the desire to dominate others. The waiter gives so that we may receive; he is emblematic of personal sacrifices that we must make in life.

WAR: Visions of war denote struggles and hardships to be faced. However, the realm of Mars is not one to be feared. War is (like winter) destructive but it makes way for the new by extinguishing the old, thus creative evolution continues on unabated. Defeat is, as the name suggests, associated with personal sadness just as visions of victory herald glad tiding and profit.

WATCH: In the framework of eternity what exactly is time? Actually, it's a concept that we have created to measure the total knowable span of our lives, in order to try and make sense of the mystery of human consciousness. The watch is representative of passing life (time) and evolution, both individual and on a wider cultural scale.

WEASEL: Frequently a sign of deceit and dishonour, but may also mark persistence and determination. The truth of the weasel's meaning rests with other clues that surround it in the vision. Observe what kinds of animals, people, situations etc. are to be found in its company.

WHALE: Awesome symbol of what resides in the deepest parts of the human mind. Any vision that rises out of the mysterious dark waters of the sea (the subconscious) is to be taken seriously for here we find the essence of existence. The whale represents order in the vast uncharted waters of the mind. It may arrive as a timely warning of important events to come. Alternatively, it can herald fear of the unknown that we do not wish to face.

WHEEL: Ancient sign of life, continuity, infinity and fertility. A circular image as is the life-giving sun. Its link with continuity stems from its constant forward motion. The wheel connects with the circle that has no beginning and no end, infinity. Any progressive symbol may be linked with sexuality and fruitfulness. The wheel can be taken as an emblem of transport. The wheel may also signify the passage time, or fear of old age.

WOODPECKER: Picus (the Roman god of agriculture) whilst out hunting one day in the forest, came across the magical goddess Circe, daughter of Sol. She fell deeply in love with the handsome Picus, but alas, the god could not return her feeling as he was already betrothed to Canens, daughter of the double-faced god of doorways, Janus. Circe's anger was fierce at this refusal, and she turned him into a woodpecker. Legend has it that Picus was so outraged by his fate that he flew into the trees and began pecking off the bark. Life is in fact not static; it is always altering and changing form. The woodpecker is a sign that your life may soon be about to alter in dramatic fashion.

WREN: Mystery, magic and legend surround the little 'Jenny wren'. The druidic priests of the Celts considered it to be a bird of divination. In ancient folklore, the wren is considered to be the bird of the waning year, whilst the robin is his (waxing year) opponent. The wren once personified the waning year and people used to hunt it at Yule, a symbolic casting-out of the old year in order to make way for the new. Vestiges of this old custom are still found in Ireland where children gather on St Stephen's Day (26th December) to make merry and visit neighbours' houses for reward. They are known as the "Wren Boys" because they carry with them the image of a wren. The wren and robin are plainly substitutes for light and dark aspects of the Sun God who is slain then reborn at summer and winter solstice. The wren remains as a symbol of change and transformation.

YACHT: A simple emblem of fair dealings and the desire to escape everyday tedium. This sign is a herald of good things coming your way and ambitions going according to plan. Time to go forth and prosper.

ZEBRA: The old striped horse of the African veldt is to be viewed in a similar context as the common horse, though the zebra is to the horse what the wildcat is to the domestic tabby. This wilder cousin of the horse denotes unbridled energy. Its striped coat associates it with the dual aspects of creation. Altogether an excellent symbol of progress.

ZOO: The dangers inherent in savage beasts have been tamed or at least contained within this place. Because of this, the zoo is symbolic of those personal fears and anxieties which we have learnt to control or ignore on a daily basis. Feeding the animals at a zoo is to understand our own emotions and denotes a certain maturity. If a wild animal escapes then beware for this is a sign that illness, gloom or deceit is at hand. With this image, much depends on the type of animal encountered.

Appendix 5
Cards

Playing cards, especially the face cards, represent quintessential aspects of the human condition. The following list may prove helpful to readers, although the subject itself is open to personal interpretation. Viewing a card as positively or negatively aspected is open to individual reading.

KING OF HEARTS: Authority, albeit connected with an emotional state of mind. Romantic involvements are indicated. In the negative aspect, it serves as a warning of marriage rifts and love squabbles.

KING OF DIAMONDS: Authority, but belonging to the realms of earthly matters such as current relationships, business ventures and financial position; also worldly events.

KING OF SPADES: Represents that which is manifest in physical form or is soon to become so; a stern and no-nonsense figure who expects discipline and obedience from those belonging to his entourage. Also, a warning that health matters should be watched with care. A threatening man.

KING OF CLUBS: Creative situations are indicated with this symbol. Expect advice (either good or bad) relating to important matters related to inspiration or artistic endeavours.

QUEEN OF HEARTS: Like the king of this suit, she is emblematic of matters close to the heart. She stands for affection, grace, true love and exciting new romance.

QUEEN OF DIAMONDS: This lady brings us good news from the Goddess herself. She represents all that is fruitful in manifest earthly form. This queen indicates wealth residing in (or coming to) the social and cultural side of your life.

QUEEN OF SPADES: She is the strict school mistress, the sad widow, the vitriolic landlady and the trenchant mother. This queen is a personification of the dark side of the feminine which is just as essential as the lighter half. She is the Cold Hag of Winter and the purifying East Wind which drives away all that stands in her icy path.

QUEEN OF CLUBS: Here is a vision of great new beginnings. She forms a bridge between the known and unknown planes. The Queen of Clubs is the illumination needed to surmount obstacles that may seem too difficult to conquer at first.

JACK OF HEARTS: A vital person filled with love for life and others. He is the good friend, the kind brother and the loyal lover. One should expect an important blessing to arrive soon after he appears.

JACK OF DIAMONDS: A materialistic sign, although not in any derogatory way. He is very much a messenger from the gods, bringing news from higher-levels so that we may have greater awareness.

JACK OF SPADES: This card represents the pioneer and the adventurer. Action all the way and new exciting opportunities can be expected when this image appears to you. There is, however, sometimes a warning in this card that health matters should not be overlooked.

JACK OF CLUBS: A fiery sign that links with everything that is energetic and full of exuberance; a herald that tells us to "go for it." Any important endeavour that has been delayed should now be launched 'full steam ahead'. Don't put off any new business, social or romantic enterprises any longer. Now is the time to take action and win the day.

CARDS AND THE TAROT
It is worth remembering that the modern pack of playing cards links closely with the ancient mystery that we know today as the Tarot.

- Hearts = Cups
- Diamonds = Pentacles and Coins
- Spades = Swords
- Clubs = Wands and Staves

HEARTS are always represented with a concave or cup-shaped dorsal surface. The idea of cupping and holding connects with the maternal image and love. Like emotions, waters flow, so it is easy to see why hearts and cups are connected. With hearts we are dealing with more astral levels of reality. We are talking of emotions and feelings that have not as yet developed into solid physical matter.

DIAMONDS - are found in the bosom of Mother Earth, they are hard shiny and beautiful. Their hardness links with the logical, conscious mind that operates within the bounds of the earth plane. Coins connect with everyday things and remind us of existing worldliness. Pentacles fit into this equation too. They are usually fashioned from metals and represent the earth element on the witch's altar. Diamonds, pentacles and coins represent solid reality and manifest creation.

SPADES - move earth and therefore alter an important aspect of reality. Spades and swords cut through air, an element that they usually represent. Thus they cut through ideas and indecision, bringing light where before only darkness reigned. However, some adepts feel safer with swords under the element of fire. The air-cutting sword and the earth-delving spade bring the material world into sharp focus. The unknown becomes knowable when this sharp sign comes into view.

CLUBS - are fashioned out of wood, a natural substance that burns, inadvertently feeding and nourishing the earth from whence it originated. We see here why confusion sometimes occurs as to which element clubs, or should we say wands, are really connected to. The fire aspect connects to the idea of brightly illuminated thought and intelligence. The club/ wand is the partner of hearts because their lessons apply to the spiritual rather than material planes. Both hearts and clubs connect with the emotions, but clubs refer more to pure adventure, rather than the passion of hearts and cups.

- Hearts and cups: love and emotion and the maternal - Venus
- Diamonds and pentacles: the earth and the physical   -   Mars
- Spades and swords: etheric link between the manifest and astral - Jupiter
- Clubs and wands: intellect, spirit and originality   - Mercury

Endnotes

a   It is in Germany that Freya's assimilation with Frigga seems to have originated. In other northern countries, particularly Denmark, Sweden, Iceland and Norway, there is good reason to believe that she was perceived as being an altogether different deity.

b   Contemporary medical observations have proved that additional breasts (polymastia) or extra nipples (polythelia) are quite common, so Hopkins and his devout colleagues probably had no shortage of targets on which to practice their arts.

c   Hell was an adopted name from Hel, Teutonic Goddess of punishment

d   Sir Walter Scott, Letters on Demonology and Witchcraft, George Routledge and Sons, London, 1884

e   Alfred's laws were actually a collection of laws that he inherited from Offa of Mercia, Ethelbert of Kent and Ine of Wessex.

f   Brythonic colonies arriving here in around 400 BCE

g   Steve Mason, professor of classics, history and religious studies at York University in Toronto (Bible Review, Feb. 2000, p. 36)

h   See: *A Layman's Guide to Who Wrote the Books of the Bible* by C. Jack Trickler, AuthorHouse (January 2, 2007), *A Feminist Companion to Luke* by Amy-Jill Levine, published by Pilgrim pr, 2004, *Marian Appearances Around the World* by Michael Donahue. Michael Donahue is a social psychologist and psychologist of religion. http://www.nhne.com/features/mary.html

i   Professor Richard Dawkins, The God Delusion, Bantam Books 2006

j   '*The Jesus Puzzle*' by Earl Doherty. 1999 Canadian Humanist Publications, *The Bible Unmasked* by Joseph Lewis, New York, The Freethought Publishing Co., Inc. Publishers, Copyright, 1926, *Did Jesus Exist?* by Frank R. Zindler, The American Atheist, Summer 1998.

k   -Jeffery L. Sheler, *The Four Gospels*, (U.S. News & World Report, Dec. 10, 1990)

l   Nachman Ben-Yehuda (Dean of the Faculty of Sociology at the Hebrew University in Jeruslalem) http://www.jewishmag.com/86mag/masada/masada.htm

m   Contemporary psychology would seem to substantiate this ancient wisdom when we look at illnesses like schizophrenia and various other forms of derangement which stem from the disturbed mind. The conscious and sub-conscious must work in unison for complete physical and mental and spiritual health and wellbeing to continue.

n   Today, this personal deity has been somewhat adulterated by New

Ageism into what has come to be called the higher-self. The nearest monotheists can get to it is the guardian angel, a sentinel watching over a person's welfare.

o   Just imagine the hullabaloo if some brave soul suggested that Christ be changed into a mortal heroic figure, or the Immaculate Virgin converted into the Queen of Holland, Germany or Sweden. Pagans have had to swallow centuries of misleading Christian-based propaganda and disinformation about their traditions, customs and sacred beliefs.

p   Incidentally, modern Druids (Celtic Priests) must remember that stone circles and other megalithic structures of worship, were built by a race far older than the Celtic one.

q   I have a feeling that one day modern science and medicine will catch up on this occult wisdom and realise that many mentally ill people are victims of damage to this psychic filter. The old adage 'away with the fairies', referring to the insane, may hold more true here than we often fully realise.

r   Whether this psychic inheritance has come down to us via genetic or past-life memory is open to speculation -the truth of the matter probably lies somewhere in the middle of the two.

s   It should be noted here that some scholars have linked the mysterious Lancelot to the Gaelic cultural hero Cuchulainn, the son of the god Lugh and a mortal maiden called Dechtir; the concept of divine impregnation is nothing new.

t   Contemporary Pagans and Witches still give veneration to the God and Goddess by remembering this ancient libation to the Old Gods during their celebrations.

THE ELDRITCH WORLD

By Nigel Pennick

The Eldritch World is a place redolent of the quality of strangeness and wonder with a seeming immunity to the passing of time; a place where there is no separation of humans and animals, and humans have the power of understanding the language of birds and beasts. Here, we shall walk the trackways of the mythological landscapes where we may encounter the malign and beneficent, the archaic and the arcane, the masked and the spectral, the formless, faceless and nameless. We shall visit the Weird Lady of the Woods, hide with King Charles in the Royal Oak and frequent the crossroads under the raven wings of night. Dare you take the first step on a journey from which there may be no return?

"Few books have been written specifically about the Otherworld...very highly recommended." Michael Howard, The Cauldron Magazine

£10.95 ISBN 978-0-9547534-3-6

For details and special offers visit www.learbooks.co.uk

THE PATH OF THE
SHAMAN
By Anna Franklin

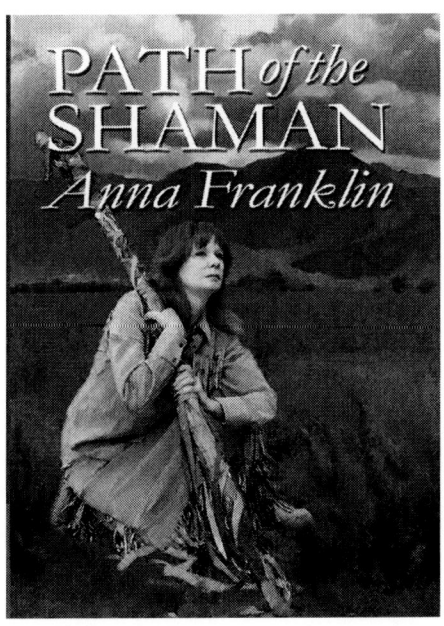

The Path of the Shaman is book two in Anna Franklin's *Eight Paths of Magic* series, exploring the role of the shaman, the mediator between the world of humankind and the world of spirits. This book explores, from the perspective of native British shamanism, the shamanic cosmos, the web of power, the shamanic crisis and becoming a shaman, healing and soul work, as well as working with the spirits of the land, plus animal and plant allies.

"I was moved beyond words by the beginning of this book. It reminded me of my traumatic numinous experiences which I have studiously tried to forget. It woke in me those vestiges of that path which I did not wish to traverse. I learned more, understood more and recognized more than I had before."
New Moon Reviews

£12.95 ISBN 978-0-9547534-4-3

For details and special offers visit www.learbooks.co.uk

HEARTH WITCH
By Anna Franklin

Book one in the *Eight Paths of Magic Series*, this book is about walking the talk. The Hearth Witch sees the sacred within the physical, the magical in the mundane, and uses this knowledge to incorporate spiritual practice into her everyday life. The way of the Hearth Witch is an uncomplicated, direct form of magic, deceptively simple and unspeakably profound. A Hearth Witch is drawn to the traditional ways, the rhythms of nature and the call of the wildwoods. The Hearth Witch of today inherits the mantle of the village wise woman or cunning man. Hers are the Old Ways of the countryside, once passed down from mother to daughter, father to son, crone to apprentice. Herbs have always been part of the wise woman's armoury. A girl was initiated into the secrets of these family formulas by her mother, along with her knowledge of folklore, stories, healing potions, brewing and wine making, fortune telling and cookery know-how. Discover these secrets and the magic of the cunning woman in *Hearth Witch*.

"A surprising amount is packed into this volume - including the history, mythology, and folklore of the hearth witch. But mostly the book concerns the practical magic of the hearth. There are few "spells" here. Instead, there are recipes for seasonal dishes (all vegetarian), for incenses and dyes, for traditional natural toiletries and cleaning products. And there is advice on raising plants, storing and preserving produce, the uses of different woods, and candle making. Only a few generations ago, such knowledge was the inheritance of every woman. The traditional wise woman was also a master of the healing arts, and over a quarter of this book is devoted to "wort cunning" (or "knowledge of herbs" to use the more familiar Latinate words). The numerous ways of preparing herbs are explained, and a lengthy directory describes the uses of many common herbs. Necessarily this is only an introduction to the vast subject of herb lore, and the bibliography contains pointers to more in-depth studies (including Anna Franklin's own tome *Herb Craft*). All in all, this is an excellent source book for all 21st Century pagans, which I for one will be referring to time and again." Libra Aries

£11.95 ISBN 978-0-9547534-1-2

For details and special offers visit www.learbooks.co.uk

NATURAL MAGIC
By Nigel Pennick

Natural magic is the way to work in harmony with the natural energies and forces that surround us all. Practising natural magic involves simple but effective practical techniques that all can use to become closer to the natural order of which we are all part. In this comprehensive introduction to natural magic, Nigel Pennick, author of 48 books on European traditional spirituality and folk-lore, provides us with an accessible in-depth approach to this most basic form of magic. The contents include an explanation of earth, mineral and plant magic; the magic of landscape and place; magical animals and how we can work with them; the power within the human body; natural magical charms, talismans and amulets, food and drink, and how to make and empower them.

"This is a welcome new edition with illustrations by the author. It teaches the reader how to work in harmony with the natural forces and elemental powers that surround us. It gives simple, yet effective, techniques to do this and many are based on the traditional witch ways known in east Anglia as the Nameless Arte...Highly recommended." Michael Howard, The Cauldron Magazine

£9.95 ISBN 978-0-9547534-2-9

For details and special offers visit www.learbooks.co.uk